ADVANCE

Timely book that gives hel[...] [...] help physicians and surgeons navigate the complex field of medicine. Doctors are well trained in medicine. The long hours and years needed to complete formal education and residency leaves physicians less prepared for the many items that invade personal time. This leaves limited personal time and leads to burnout. This book will benefit many physicians

- Dr. Linda Leffel, MD, plastic surgeon

"The Doctor Dilemma" by Dr. Sara Dill is truly a Doctor's self help book that contains many practical tools throughout its pages. It presents and inspires the reader to introspectively examine and come to terms with finding out why they aren't happy or fulfilled in their chosen career. It further suggests steps to take that encourages one to discover those positive qualities and goals of being in this profession.

This book is filled with ingenious, but simple to follow techniques, that will guide the reader to finding their own way out of their doctor dilemma.

- Jim Hickey (non MD)

I wish I had this book four years ago when I was experiencing my own difficult career transition as a physician. Dr. Dill's book is incredibly relatable to most physicians who feel trapped in a chaotic medical system. The medical analogies made it feel like I was having a conversation instead of reading.

Thank you, Dr. Dill, for shedding light on what has been known but rarely openly discussed in the medical field!

- Dr. Uzma Khan, MD

If you have ever doubted if a career in medicine was the right choice for you then you MUST read this book! Dr. Dill draws, both from her personal experiences and her experiences as a life coach for unhappy physicians, to create a roadmap to discover joy and purpose in your life. She provides practical tips and strategies that, if followed, will lead to greater contentment. This book should be on the bookshelf of every doctor and should be referred to frequently when times get hard and you feel like quitting. This book is a true gem!

- Dr. Thandeka Myeni MD MPH

Dr. Sara Dill's sensitive and thoughtfully written book is a timely address to those physicians who entered a caring profession, only to encounter corporate number crunching and depersonalization. Anyone with a soul that feels lost in

American society 2018 would benefit from an encounter with Dr. Dill's ponderings and suggestions. Perfect timing.

- Dr. Karen Vaniver, MD, plastic surgeon

I felt it hit on a lot of topics that have been on my mind as well as my colleagues when we discuss 'burnout' that is so prevalent among physicians. Whether you choose to stay in your current position, elect to search for another, or even choose to look for a career outside of medicine, this book is there to help you navigate the way.

- Dr. Amanda Parker, M.D., F.A.C.S.

Sara's book is great for someone who is in need of a change and some advice. But I promise you it is also perfect for someone who wants to stay in love and passionate with Medicine and with being a doctor!

The Doctor Dilemma is well written, has a great flow to it. The motivational quotes throughout the book are a plus! I have written them randomly on my daily planner!

- Dr. Alice Gallo de Moraes, MD, Pulmonary and Critical Care Medicine

The Doctor Dilemma

THE
DOCTOR
DILEMMA

How to Quit Being Miserable Without Quitting Medicine

SARA DILL, MD

NEW YORK

LONDON • NASHVILLE • MELBOURNE • VANCOUVER

The Doctor Dilemma

How to Quit Being Miserable Without Quitting Medicine

Published in New York, New York, by Morgan James Publishing in partnership with Difference Press. Morgan James is a trademark of Morgan James, LLC. www.MorganJamesPublishing.com

ISBN 9781642792454 paperback
ISBN 9781642792461 eBook
Library of Congress Control Number: 2018910390

Cover Design by:
Rachel Lopez
www.r2cdesign.com

Interior Design by:
Chris Treccani
www.3dogcreative.net

Morgan James is a proud partner of Habitat for Humanity Peninsula and Greater Williamsburg. Partners in building since 2006.

Get involved today! Visit
MorganJamesPublishing.com/giving-back

To my family and friends, who always believed in me, even when I didn't fully believe in myself. Thank you. I love you dearly.

TABLE OF CONTENTS

Introduction

*"You will be pushed by pain until
you are pulled by vision."*

– Michael Beckwith

This book is for you. I wrote it to help doctors who feel like I did several years ago: unhappy, burned out, and confused about whether to keep practicing or not. This book is what I wish I had available to me when I was struggling with not liking my career as a physician and secretly wondering whether I had made a mistake in even going to medical school. At the time, I felt so alone and so confused. I just wanted to understand why I wasn't happy as a doctor, why I didn't like my job, and what to do about it. I spent a lot of time wondering whether I should stay in my current practice or leave, whether I should leave medicine altogether, and what I was truly wanting in life (and why I didn't have it). Maybe you feel similar? Like you should be happier as a doctor but you don't really like your current job or career in general? Maybe you are totally burned out already and in survival mode, struggling to decide whether to quit your job or try to make it work a little longer. Or maybe you are in a job that makes you miserable and you don't know what to do. If so, there are answers here for you.

This book is based on what I have learned through intensive study and experimentation on myself over the last five years. I have read hundreds of books, attended many classes and workshops and retreats, completed two life coach training programs, and spent tens of thousands of dollars on the process. Through personal experimentation, and lots of mistakes, I have refined what works and what doesn't work to go from being an unhappy, dissatisfied doctor to feeling better, understanding what is missing in your life and career, and having a plan to get it. This book is also based on my work with real-life burned-out physician clients. It discusses the exact tools and steps I use to help my clients understand what's causing their unhappiness, burnout, and career dissatisfaction and how to fix it. This book can help you too – and it won't take years or cost you lots of mistakes!

If you are reading, it means you're probably not happy in your current practice. You might even be wondering deep inside whether you made a mistake becoming a doctor. My guess is you feel confused, stuck, sad, hopeless, and probably a little angry. Right? After all those years of school and residency, why is being a doctor not what you expected it to be? Why is it so hard, and when does it get easier? And what can you do about it?

I get it. I *totally* get it. I have been there myself, and I've worked with many other physicians who were really unhappy in medicine and well down the road to burnout, and who didn't even know it. So many doctors, myself included, don't realize that they are burned out. They think they are just tired and unhappy and don't enjoy their medical practice anymore. I really get how awful it feels to hate your job and especially to question the very career you spent so many years training for and worked so hard to get.

Let me tell you a bit about me and my story. Like you, I excelled in school. I worked hard and studied a lot, but I enjoyed school and did well. I grew up in California but always wanted to be a New Englander. I went to Harvard University for my undergraduate education, and then attended the University of California San Diego School of Medicine.

Medical school was tough, but I also really enjoyed it. I had to study almost all the time. The first two years of medical school were difficult, especially as a non-science major. But the clinical years were so much better! Scary – yes. Outside my comfort zone – yes. A challenge every day – yes. But I loved most of my rotations and really loved helping patients and learning so much. Instead of going into pediatrics as I had planned, I fell in love with dermatology, especially pediatric dermatology. What about you? Did you enjoy medical school, even with its challenges, or perhaps even then you had doubts about whether it was the right choice for you?

I matched into (remember the tension?) the Dermatology Training Program at Brown Medical School and was excited to move back to New England. Residency was challenging though. Although dermatology residency is less time-consuming in terms of clinical hours than some other residencies, the amount of time a resident is expected to study and work outside of clinical training is quite high. I found it hard to have any sort of work-life balance as a resident, although I did my best. And sometimes I really didn't enjoy my workdays. Everyone else seemed to love it so much more than I did. (I know now that wasn't true, but it seemed true at the time. This was one of many times that I compared what I was feeling and thinking on the inside to what other people were saying and doing on the outside.) I didn't realize that many medical (and even dermatology) residents sometimes wondered whether they made the right choice. I still excelled and was a co-chief resident during my last year.

After graduating, I worked in a variety of academic settings and even went back into training to complete a fellowship in pediatric dermatology. I also worked for Kaiser Permanente for a year and had a brief stint in private practice. But I wasn't loving my career, even though I was only a few years into it. And I didn't know what to do. Here I was, in dermatology, a field typically considered one of the "happier" specialties, working four days a week, earning a good living, and yet I wasn't happy – and I didn't feel fulfilled by my work. I started wondering whether I had made a mistake in becoming a dermatologist. What was wrong with me that I wasn't happier? And what should I do about it? I couldn't imagine twenty or thirty more years of practice. But I didn't know what else I could do or even what I might want to do. I worried I had wasted all that time in school and training. I worried about what people would say. I didn't want to disappoint my friends and family and my mentors. And I needed to support myself financially. I was terrified and felt trapped and alone and stuck. I didn't know anyone who felt the same way, and I didn't know what to do.

I got a clue, however, when I returned to Brown as the dermatology residency program director. The position let me split my time between an academic pediatric dermatology clinical practice with residents and students, and the administrative role of residency program director. I enjoyed the residency program director part of my job. I *loved* helping residents and faculty solve problems, communicate better, and make decisions about their career plans and life in general. And I was really good at it. I also liked my pediatric dermatology clinics, but never as much as my nonclinical duties. Sigh. So I was sort of stuck. I wondered whether this was normal. Was this as good as it was going to get? I worked four days a week and mostly liked what I did. My patients were lovely people. But I found I didn't want to talk to them about their skin. I wanted to talk to them about their lives.

So, I did what I always do when I need to figure something out: I looked to books to help me. I read a lot of them! Some helped. Some didn't. Then I took classes. Then I went on retreats. I became more and more clear that I really wanted to take a break from medicine and figure it all out. I saved up enough to support myself for a year and took a sabbatical. But I still didn't know what to do or what the problem really was.

Slowly, I figured it out. I discovered this thing called life coaching and completed a nine-month training program with Martha Beck, Oprah's *O Magazine* life coach. In learning to be a life coach, you basically coach yourself and get coached nonstop. I finally got answers and started to understand why I had struggled so much in my medical career and how I had (unintentionally) made my unhappiness so much worse.

Much of my career dissatisfaction came not from the challenges of practicing medicine and caring for patients but from what I was thinking and believing about those things, and that affected how I showed up in my career. I learned that my deep fear of making mistakes and my strong perfectionistic tendencies created the majority of the stress I felt in practice. I learned that my sense of being not good enough and worrying that I wasn't nearly as skilled as other physicians (hello, imposter syndrome) prevented me from finding more satisfaction and joy in my career. I learned that trying to make everyone happy, and to have everyone like me, including patients, friends, family, and even strangers, was sabotaging my happiness. This was a big part of why I felt like I was living someone else's life and not my own. I also realized that my unwillingness to disappoint other people (and, instead, to disappoint myself) was preventing me from doing what I truly wanted to do. And that all of my medical training, especially the emphasis on *always* putting patients first, had exacerbated all these tendencies I already had. No wonder I didn't thrive in my medical career! Of course I was getting burned out and not enjoying my dermatology practice. I never had a chance at happiness and career satisfaction.

My coaches have helped me so much. (And still do.) I completed a second life coach training program to really hone my skills, and I fell more and more in love with this profession. I realized I had essentially been acting as a life coach during my residency program director days and that this was what I wanted to do full-time. And, of course, the people I wanted to help were my fellow physicians. Could I go back and practice dermatology again and be happy? Yes. Absolutely. I now have the knowledge and skills to find happiness and fulfillment in any career I choose. But for now, I am happily a life coach for unhappy physicians.

You are my people. You are who I was always meant to help. I am still a doctor. I just practice now in another way. This way. Are you ready to figure out what you are truly wanting in your career and life and how to get it? Do you want to learn how to feel better along the way?

Let's go!

CHAPTER 1

Telling Yourself
the Truth

"There are no mistakes in life, only lessons. There is no such thing as a negative experience, only opportunities to grow, learn, and advance along the road of self-mastery."

– ROBIN SHARMA

I want to congratulate you on having the courage to acknowledge that you are not happy and that you want more than the career and life you currently have. It's not easy to admit to yourself that you might have made a mistake in choosing your current job or, worse, in even becoming a doctor. Allowing yourself to ask these questions, even if you tell no one else, can be very frightening and unsettling. It may make you question your judgment about anything and everything.

This is okay. This is normal. It may not feel okay, but I promise you, it is.

I've been there. I've worked with many other doctors who felt exactly the same way. And I can help you figure out what to do about it.

What do you think being courageous feels like? Many of us have this idea that being courageous must feel good. It doesn't. Courage is defined by the *Oxford Dictionary* as "the ability to do something that frightens one." Courage is being terrified and doing something anyway. Courage is asking yourself the hard questions whose answers you are reluctant (or afraid) to discover. It is acknowledging that although your life might look good or even *amazing* on paper, it doesn't feel good to you. It is asking for help when you need it. Courage is taking action even when you aren't sure it's the right thing to do. You *are* courageous. Really. And I want to help you see that in yourself.

The recognition that you aren't happy is the first step toward having a life that does bring you happiness. Isn't it odd how we pretend to ourselves that we are happy? As if we can keep how we are feeling a secret from ourselves. What other secrets are you trying to keep yourself from knowing about your career and life? Creating any type of lasting change in our lives starts with being honest with ourselves. The process begins with gently turning toward what we know to be true and allowing ourselves to acknowledge what is not working in our lives. You don't have to tell anyone else. Just yourself.

Whatever you are feeling right now is totally normal. I don't know about you, but no one ever told me that life was going to be so hard and confusing for so long. Sadly, our lives don't come with a manual or cheat sheet. I mean, really, we humans need a user's guide! I thought the hard part of being a doctor was getting into a good college, and then getting accepted to and completing medical school, and then surviving residency. I thought once I finished residency my life would be so much better. And in some ways, it was; but in some ways, it was worse. I thought being an attending physician would be so much easier than being a resident and that I would be so much happier. I think having expectations like this is why it can be so confusing to find yourself a practicing physician and yet an unhappy one. And why it's way more common than we might think it is.

When I decided to take a break – I called it a sabbatical – from practicing dermatology, I was uncomfortable telling people, *especially* other physicians. I worried *a lot* about what they might think or say. I worried they would think I was being foolish, selfish, stupid, and short-sighted. I worried they would think I didn't know how good I had it, that I was making a big mistake, that I would regret this decision forever. Basically, I worried they would not understand what I was doing and judge me for it. (Of course, since then I have learned that whenever I am afraid of what someone else thinks or says, it is because a part of me is already thinking or saying that about myself. More on that later.)

However, what I discovered – and what I think you will discover too – is that almost all doctors I spoke with confessed to wishing they could do what I was doing. They all told me of their dreams of time off, travel, more time for hobbies, more time with family and friends. Many of them sincerely enjoyed practicing medicine, but every doctor I spoke with also wished for more freedom and more time to do everything else they wanted to do in life.

What I began to realize then, and what I know for sure now after working with many unhappy physicians, is that we all have doubts. We all have thoughts about the life we might have had if only we had made different choices. Maybe some of us have more doubts than others. Maybe there is a rare doctor out there who has never doubted her choice of medicine, or type of practice, ever. Even on a bad day. And I am so happy for her. That's wonderful. But I haven't met her yet.

These days it is harder to find a completely happy doctor than to find an unhappy one. Right? You've probably seen the articles. You've talked to your colleagues. The burnout rate continues to rise across all medical specialties. Yes, even in my specialty, dermatology. Physicians no longer have only to contend with the inherent stress of caring for patients; we now have to deal with EMRs, insurance companies, declining reimbursements, increasing administrative oversight, loss of autonomy, and so on. Physicians everywhere are feeling this squeeze.

So, I encourage you to start right now to treat yourself as you would a scared or confused patient. Speak softly to yourself. Ask questions kindly and gently. Be curious. What's going on with you? You probably keep telling yourself "I don't know." The voice in your head might sound like:

"I don't know what's wrong with me."

"I don't know why I am so unhappy."

"I don't know if I made a mistake taking this job or becoming a doctor."

"I don't know what to do."

That's what I mean about telling yourself a lot of "I don't know." But "I don't know" will keep you stuck. "I don't know" is a dream-stealer.

I want you to see if you can discover what you *do* know to be true for you right now. Keep asking. Maybe try journaling. You don't have to do anything with the answers. So much of the time, I think we don't want to know what is true because we are afraid of what it will mean; we are afraid of what we will have to do about it. You don't have to do anything about it until, and unless, you want to. Acknowledging that you hate your job (and maybe the whole medical profession) and that you don't know what to do about it is enough for now. You don't have to know anything else right now. You're just taking a history of the present illness right now. You aren't ready to formulate the diagnosis, let alone the assessment and plan.

If you don't even know how to start identifying what's wrong, and what you do know, writing prompts and coaching exercises can help. You may need to do them over and over again. Sometimes we uncover one layer of truth, and only later can we go back and discover something else we couldn't see before.

Go ahead and grab paper and pen. Take a few minutes and ask yourself the following questions. Feel free to repeat this exercise as often as you need to.

What do you like about your career and life right now? Can you make a list?

What do you dislike (or hate) about your career and life right now? Write it all down.

What are you afraid to admit to yourself about your life? Why? What else? Repeat these questions for five minutes. Just write it all down. Get it out of your head and on paper.

Why did you become a doctor? Spend some time on this. Go back and remember when you were applying to medical school or learned you were accepted. Reflect on that first day of medical school. What were your reasons, your hopes, your dreams?

Did you do the exercise? If not, don't worry about it. Maybe just spend a few minutes thinking about the answers. You don't have to write it all down right now. But it is interesting to see if anything surprises you about your answers. Maybe the only thing you really like about your job right now is the paycheck. Or maybe you still enjoy seeing patients, or certain kinds of patients, but dislike everything else about the practice of medicine these days. Or maybe there is a lot you like about your career, but you simply want to work less. This is all really good information to have.

A lot of my clients find this exercise challenging to do honestly. It's common to find yourself judging your answers or making things sound not so bad. This is normal but can get in the way of your progress. Again, this is just like taking a history from a patient. Can you step into that same curious and compassionate role you assume with patients? You need to know the facts of your own particular case to be most effective in finding the solution to your career unhappiness. And as you'll see in the next chapter, doctors are especially at risk of finding themselves in this position of being unhappy, burned out, and miserable in their careers – through no fault of their own.

CHAPTER 2

How You've Been Set Up for Unhappiness

"Human happiness and human satisfaction must ultimately come from within oneself."

– 14TH DALAI LAMA

I t's helpful and important to understand the very good reasons you are so unhappy and dissatisfied as a doctor right now. After all, just like with treating an illness, the more we understand the cause of the disease, the more likely we are to be able to cure it. Otherwise, the best we can do is simply treat the symptoms and hope it improves with time. And that may be what you have been doing. Perhaps you have been treating the symptoms of your unhappiness rather than understanding the cause of it. I did this. I was unhappy in my first job after residency, so I got a different job. I didn't love that one either,

9

so I did a fellowship. Then I got another job. And another job. Each one was better in some ways than the previous one, so there was improvement. But I was only treating the symptoms: my unhappiness, having a job I didn't love, worrying about making mistakes at work and in life, and being dissatisfied.

The first very good reason you are unhappy is that it's normal not to be happy all the time. I know, right? What kind of self-help book tells you that? Don't stop reading yet. This is actually good news! It means you are a normal human being who is experiencing some negative human emotions. In spite of what popular culture, self-help books, social media posts, psychologists, counselors, and even life coaches would have us believe, it is normal to experience a wide range of emotions, both positive and negative. Right? Hasn't that been your experience so far in life? Perhaps Byron Katie, Eckhart Tolle, and the few other fully enlightened individuals experience a constant state of contentment, but that is not my experience. Not yet, at least. Is it yours? Is there some part of you that believes that you really should be happy all the time? You may notice that you actually feel better just knowing that feeling unhappy is okay and normal and totally to be expected at times. Telling yourself you should feel happy when you don't sets you up for feeling even worse. So it can be a relief to understand that it is totally normal not to be happy all the time. And, yes, you *can* do things to feel consistently happier than you do right now. (If you are impatient to get started, check out the Two-Minute Happiness Hacks at the end of this book.)

Perhaps you have read something on the negativity bias of the human brain? It is the fact that humans give more psychological weight to bad experiences than to good ones. Research by psychologist John Gottman, as discussed in his book *Why Marriages Succeed or Fail*, reveals that it takes five positive interactions to overcome any one negative interaction. (1) This supports Dr. Rick Hanson's statement in his book *Buddha's Brain* that "the brain is like Velcro for negative experiences but Teflon for positive ones." (2) It makes sense that, to survive, it is way more important to avoid negative (and potentially lethal or dangerous) situations than it is to focus on positive experiences. Basically, if you think about how we evolved as a species, it makes sense that we evolved to be fearful. Looking for danger and focusing on potential danger very likely helped keep our ancestors alive. The fact that you are here today means that your ancestors were pretty good at spotting danger (real or imagined).

Yet now we live in a world in which most of us are not regularly in physical danger. Barring illness or accidents, for most of us the world is not nearly as threatening as the one in which we evolved. And yet our brain has not caught up. Our brain does not really care whether we are happy or not. It cares that we are alive, that we survive, and, from an evolutionary standpoint, that we pass our genes along. So when we have urges and instincts and irrational fears and stress, thank evolution and the human brain. Yes, they have gotten you here and have kept you alive. But at what cost? Left unsupervised, our brain and our thinking default to looking for problems, looking for what is wrong, looking for danger. This is sort of a bummer for those of us who want to feel happier, isn't it?

There is good news. Happiness *is* something we can foster. As a species, we need to learn how to cultivate happiness. Understanding why our default mode is one of fear and worry and looking for everything wrong is good to know. It means nothing is wrong with you. You are a normal human with a brain that is doing what it is supposed to do. But these hardwired tendencies are certainly not helping you find happiness and fulfillment in your job and career, or in life in general.

There are also personal and professional reasons why you are experiencing such dissatisfaction and unhappiness as a doctor. Some of these are what cause so much burnout and dissatisfaction among doctors these days. I like to call it "Doctor Brain." We all have it. It is the programming we got as we made our way through medical school, residency, and beyond. It's the culture of medicine that we all have taken on, often without question.

I want you to think back to medical school and to your residency. These were challenging times. Right? Especially when you remember the person you were when you showed up to class on the first day of medical school. If you are like the physicians I know, you went to medical school out of a deep desire to help people, to ease suffering, and to make a positive difference in the world. And then we were introduced to the culture of medicine. And despite some changes for the better, by and large it is still a culture in many ways similar to that of the military. I grew up with a former Navy SEAL dad who used to frequently repeat his two favorite SEAL slogans: "The only easy day was yesterday" and "Pain is just weakness leaving the body." These sayings, meant for soldiers preparing for combat, came to mind frequently during my medical training. They totally apply to medical training, don't they?

Like the military, traditional medical education relies on a rigid hierarchy of rank and responsibility. Often, attendings act less like colleagues or mentors and more like disciplinarians. In many training environments, mistakes are not viewed as opportunities for growth but rather as opportunities for humiliation. We learn not to complain, that when the going gets tough to simply work harder, never to show weakness, to suck it up, never to make mistakes, and always to put patients first. Our natural caring tendency is frequently co-opted into a feeling that we are responsible for solving every problem and that we need to "fix" our patients, even when what they have isn't "fixable." Or they don't want fixing. And most of us began medical school as sincere and hardworking individuals with an already overdeveloped sense of responsibility. Sound familiar?

Are You Burned Out and Don't Know It?

My hunch is that you are experiencing some features of burnout and may not even know it. I was working only four days a week and yet, I was getting burned out. It is not always the number of hours you work, but how you work, and the thoughts and feelings driving your work, that can lead to burnout. Burnout has three characteristics: exhaustion (both emotional and physical); depersonalization (sarcasm, cynicism, complaining about your job and patients); and lack of efficacy or loss of a sense of purpose or meaning in your work. One recent study found that 60 percent of medical students and residents experience burnout, as do 50 percent of early career physicians. (3) If you aren't burned out yet, you might be headed that way.

Many physicians don't realize that they are experiencing symptoms of burnout. Do you think feeling exhausted all the time is normal? How much do you find yourself complaining about or blaming patients or feeling cynical about your job and medicine in general? Do you feel like what you do matters or has meaning? This is important to know. Are you just surviving right now in your medical practice and calling that normal? Sadly, it is common these days, but that doesn't make it okay. The good news is that burnout is 100 percent curable.

By now I hope you feel a little better about the fact that you are unhappy and dissatisfied and unfulfilled in your job and/or career and/or life. It is almost the new normal to be an unhappy and overworked and overwhelmed physician. How are you feeling as you read all this? Is investigating and trying to understand the cause of the problem helping at all? Sometimes just beginning to look at what's wrong and why can help shift some of the fear and resistance to exploring what is really wrong and how to solve it.

And you are trying to do something about it! You are seeking to change this. There is a part of you, maybe a small, still voice inside that keeps telling you that this is not okay. Yes, it's okay to be unhappy sometimes. But not forever. Not for the next thirty years of your career. Unlike so many docs who seem to accept this as their fate, you are brave enough to want more. In reading this book, you are starting to take action and discover what you truly want and how to get it.

Chapter 3

The Path Forward

"The journey of a thousand miles begins
with one step."

– Lao Tzu

The MINDFUL Process

It took me years to figure out what I now help my clients discover in a few weeks: why you are so unhappy, how to start feeling better now (even in your current job and career), what your dream job might look like, and how to develop a clear plan to move forward to create the career and life you really want. The process I use comes from my own experience and what worked for me. And it has been shaped by learning a lot about what doesn't work, too!

This is where my personal experience can really help you and hopefully prevent you from making the same mistakes I did. I changed jobs over and over again to try to feel better and find that "perfect" job. I had six jobs in my first eight years working as a board-certified dermatologist, including several academic practices, a fellowship, and positions at a large managed care organization and in private practice. Typically, my new job *was* better, at least for a while, but soon I would be unhappy and dissatisfied, and the process would start all over. And because I didn't really understand why I was feeling unhappy or how to feel better regardless of what was happening in my life, I repeated the pattern. I kept looking for the answer outside of me. It's like dating the same kind of person over and over and blaming them each time for being a jerk. Eventually, you realize that you need to look at yourself to diagnosis the real problem. Not because there is something wrong with you but to begin to understand your patterns and investigate why you aren't getting the results you want in life.

Finally, I was so tired of being unhappy and dissatisfied that I decided to take a year off and find answers. I saved up and took a sabbatical from my dermatology practice. Although I loved the time off, I still didn't know what to do with my life. Adding up my lost salary as a dermatologist plus the money spent that I had saved, it was an expensive year off (well over

$400,000) without much to show for it. I ended up spending all that money and more before I figured out my next steps. I did try several occupations, including starting a food tour business, working for a pharmaceutical company, and training as a life coach. The food tour business was a good experience in becoming an entrepreneur, but it was the life coach training that really helped me get clarity on my career. It allowed me to finally understand how, and where, I was causing a lot of my own problems and getting in my own way. I saw how I was hoping that someone else would fix my career and life, and how I wasn't taking full responsibility for my choices, for my past, and for my future. I wanted some magic pill to make everything better. I realized I had stopped asking *me* what I really wanted and instead was just taking what was offered to me in my career. I wasn't in the driver's seat of my life – it was as if I was a passenger in the car of my life's journey. I finally understood that I needed and wanted to honor my dreams and go after them in spite of the discomfort and fear I felt.

The time I spent working full-time for a pharmaceutical company, before I started my physician coaching practice, really helped me see that it was mostly me, and not my job, that was truly causing my unhappiness. I had a lot of the same thoughts about working as a clinical dermatologist in practice as I had about being a clinical director in the pharmaceutical industry. Those thoughts sounded like: "I don't know if this is right," "I am not fulfilling my purpose," "I don't like this, maybe I should do something else," "I think I made a mistake," "I don't know enough," "I might make a mistake," "I am not smart enough," and so on. Same thoughts. Different jobs. So, instead of changing jobs again because I was unhappy, I decided to do the opposite. I decided to go all-in on my job in the pharmaceutical industry and figure out how to like it and excel. And you know what? It worked! My work improved, I learned to ask for what I wanted (like working part-time), and I showed up 100 percent. I still consult for the company part-time and have my coaching practice, too. My time there has provided such an important lesson for me on how I could feel so much better simply by changing how I thought about my job before changing the job itself.

Now I work exclusively with other physicians who are struggling with what I used to struggle with: a job they don't like, terrible work-life balance, and a medical career that they aren't sure they want. Through personal experience, working with physician clients, and combining my life coach training, background in practicing and teaching mindfulness meditation, and the hundreds of self-help books I've read over the last few years, I created the following seven-step MINDFUL process. It's a highly effective method to become a happier doctor and create a career you love. I personally use this process as I navigate my career and life and use it with all my physician clients.

The MINDFUL process includes the following steps:

1. **M**indfulness – become the observer.
2. **I**dentify your thoughts.
3. **N**avigate your feelings.
4. **D**etermine your values and priorities – live your life, not someone else's.
5. **F**uel yourself first – self-care isn't selfish.
6. **U**niquely yours – identify your dream career.
7. **L**ook out for obstacles and problem solve in advance.

Step 1: Mindfulness – Become the Observer

The first step is always to try to get a little relief from the intensity of what you are experiencing. Think about a patient in the emergency department who is terrified. You start by helping that panicked patient calm down. It can take some time and some reassurance. Often it is possible for a patient to start feeling a little relief even before you establish a clear diagnosis or begin treatment.

For my clients, developing mindfulness is the first step toward feeling better and creating an ideal career and life. What is mindfulness and how does it help? Jon Kabat-Zinn, a well-known researcher and the founder of the mindfulness-based stress reduction (MBSR) program, defines mindfulness as "the awareness that arises by paying attention on purpose, in the present moment, and nonjudgmentally." (4) Mindfulness is essentially paying attention without judging events and experiences as good or bad, positive or negative. Basically, it is observing what is happening outside of you, in the external world, and what is happening inside of you, in your internal world of thoughts, emotions, and physical sensations.

I teach my clients to start paying *more* attention to what is happening, not less. To stop fighting what is occurring in their life right now, even if they don't like it, and to get curious about what is going on and why. Especially if you aren't happy with your life, you need to lean in rather than run away. By becoming the observer of what is happening, we create some space between ourselves and what we are experiencing. And that space will often feel like a little bit of relief. For my client Dr. C., this looked like noticing when she was feeling overwhelmed or angry and taking some deep breaths. It looked like noticing when she felt rushed and overwhelmed and pausing before seeing her next patient. It also looked like noticing which aspects of her job she enjoyed (which patients or diseases or procedures she liked) and which parts she did not. Just noticing and collecting information is an integral part of the MINDFUL process.

Step 2: Identify Your Thoughts

The second step is to focus your awareness and attention on what you are thinking and believing. Our thoughts and beliefs are what create all of our feelings, and our feelings drive our actions. So, identifying what we are thinking is the key to understanding what is really wrong and how to fix it. This is the difference between treating the symptoms a patient presents with versus using those symptoms to determine the underlying diagnosis so that you can cure the patient for good. For example, my client Dr. B. noticed her internal dialogue every morning about how much she hated her job and how bad the day was going to be. These thoughts were on repeat and then started a chain reaction, causing more thoughts about how she had made a big mistake becoming a doctor and how much time she had wasted and that she didn't know what to do now. These thoughts seemed true to her. Of course they did! She repeated them every day. But by observing her thinking as thinking, and realizing that these thoughts were just sentences in her head, she began to see why she was miserable and stressed out about her day even before she got out of the shower.

This is like a patient who comes in with an itchy rash. I could simply treat it by giving the patient topical or oral steroids. But unless I know the cause of the rash, it is likely to recur or my treatment might make it worse. This is why I tell all my clients not to quit their job too soon, and especially not to make a decision to leave medicine altogether, until they understand how they got to this point in their life and what the underlying issues really are. Your current job is the itchy rash. You don't like it. It's uncomfortable and you want relief now. Just like giving topical steroids may be the right treatment for a pruritic eruption from poison ivy but is the wrong treatment for a fungal infection, quitting medicine may indeed treat the apparent symptoms but may not be necessary or best for you. You won't know until you diagnose the underlying problem.

Step 3: Navigate Your Feelings

The next step is observing and understanding what you are feeling and why you are feeling the way you do. This is the step my physician clients tend to protest about the most and want to skip. It is also the key step for making any lasting change in your life. Everything we do is because of what we want or don't want to feel. Developing awareness of your emotions and ways to deal with the uncomfortable ones is a skill you need to create the life you truly want. For Dr. K., this involved using an app on his phone to remind him to check in and notice how he was feeling during the day. By building the muscle of attention, my clients become more aware of how they are feeling and notice how emotions actually feel in their bodies, how feelings come and go, and how they can respond to them in skillful or unskillful ways.

Step 4: Determine Your Values and Priorities – Live Your Life, Not Someone Else's

The fourth step is one of my favorites. This is where my clients start to identify their values and priorities. So often, what they discover is that a major reason they are dissatisfied with their job and career is because they are not living a life that is in accord with their personal values and what is truly important to them. They are living without integrity. Dr. R. recognized that a full social life and connection to people were important to her and that she had not been making time for either of these. Incorporating into her daily life opportunities to feel more connected with others – starting with patients and colleagues at work – made a huge difference for her right away, and she also focused on the longer-term goal of making new friends in her new job and city.

Step 5: Fuel Yourself First – Self-Care Isn't Selfish

The fifth step in the MINDFUL process is identifying what you need to be at your best and learning how to make sure you take care of yourself *first* rather than *last*. This might include getting seven or eight hours of sleep at night or going to the gym or a yoga class regularly. This might look like eating healthy foods or taking a lunch break. It might include hiring a housecleaner or having a date night every week with your spouse or partner. Or this might look like learning to ask better questions of yourself. As physicians, we are wonderful at taking care of everyone around us. But we tend to be terrible at taking care of ourselves unless it is an emergency. This was hard for a resident client of mine, Dr. D. She didn't want to acknowledge that she needed seven to eight hours of sleep at night to feel good. By realizing that getting enough sleep helped her to perform better and be more productive – it made it easier for her to prioritize sleep and her own well-being – and structure her work and life to set herself up for success.

Step 6: Uniquely Yours – Identify Your Dream Career

More often than not, most physicians have only a vague sense of what they truly want out of their medical career. We are so used to making the best of things and not complaining that, after we finish our training, we often just accept what we are offered.

Or we compromise without even asking for what we want. This is especially true if you are a female physician. This step is about identifying what you really, *really* want. It requires you to focus on your future and what you want to have rather than focusing on the past and what you don't have. Your dream future will (absolutely) seem impossible, and so typically we don't let ourselves even acknowledge what we secretly wish for. But identifying your ideal workday, whether it includes seeing patients, is essential to creating a concrete step-by-step plan for making your "too-good-to-be-true" dreams come true. Dr. A.'s ideal job was working four full days a week as a surgeon, taking all weekends and nights off, and not taking any call. She wanted more time with her family *and* a successful medical practice. Often, we think we have to choose. My job as a physician coach is to point out where you are settling for less than what you really want and to help you find ways to have it all, as much as possible.

Step 7: Look Out for Obstacles and Problem Solve in Advance

In this final step, you list all the possible reasons why you might not be able to achieve the dream career (and life) you identified in step six. There will always be obstacles and roadblocks in achieving anything worthwhile. This is especially true when you are creating a dream career and other wildly impossible life goals. But after you identify all the potential problems you might face, you come up with potential solutions for each and every obstacle. In doing this, your dream starts to seem less impossible and the path forward becomes clearer.

These steps might seem too simple. And they are simple. But they are not easy. We absolutely can change our lives by first changing our patterns of thinking, feeling, and behaving, but it takes time and determination. It is much easier to simply settle for the status quo and what you see around you. But I know you want more. I want you to have more. Your desires are important. Your dreams are important. They are the guides for all that your life can be.

> *"The future belongs to those who believe in the beauty of their dreams."*
>
> – Eleanor Roosevelt

CHAPTER 4

Begin Where You Are

"We deal with our mind from morning to evening, and it can be our best friend or our worst enemy."

– MATTHIEU RICARD

Step 1: Mindfulness – Become the Observer

When I start working with my clients, they are always in such a hurry to feel better. I get it. It feels terrible to feel terrible. And each one is convinced that the way to feel better *now* is to "fix" something or change something: their job, their career, where they live, maybe their relationships. I know this feeling of urgency. After all, when you dislike your job and are questioning the very career you spent years pursuing, it feels like an emergency. It feels overwhelming. It feels incredibly painful and frightening. And we want to feel better immediately!

I want you to compare your current career problems to the situation of a patient being seen in the emergency department. Patients come into the ED with any number of symptoms, which may be caused by countless kinds of illness or trauma. They are experiencing a range of symptoms. They are also scared and anxious and may even be in a panic. This is understandable, right? But is it helpful? No. Your job as a physician assessing a patient is to ascertain what is really urgent or emergent and what is not. Your job is to figure out what the underlying problem is and then how to treat it. Your job is also to relieve the patient's pain as much as possible even before treating the cause of it.

Patients' fear and anxiety and sense of urgency, though understandable, often exacerbate the actual pain and suffering they are experiencing from their underlying illness or accident. This is likely what is happening to you. The underlying problem you have may be a job or career you don't like, but the degree of confusion and panic and fear you are experiencing about not liking your medical career is what is deepening your unhappiness. Urgency is always a sign to slow down. You can't make good decisions from a place of urgency and unhappiness.

This is also why doctors don't typically treat themselves or family members, and especially not in emergency situations. You are too close. You can't be objective. You can't see the details because you are too swept up in your own fears and worries. This is exhausting, too.

Dr. F. was in her first year of work after completing a very competitive residency and fellowship. She came to me because she was miserable and angry and confused, and she had no idea what had gone wrong. She just knew this was not what she wanted. She told me she had a terrible job, she was exhausted all the time, she felt totally trapped and miserable, and she felt as if her whole life was a disaster. To her, her life felt completely unsustainable and like an emergency. To me, I could see a very different picture – the big picture. I saw a smart and successful young doctor with so many options available to her. I saw a physician who officially worked four days a week but who was having problems with efficiency, leaving work late, and bringing work home with her. I saw a brilliant clinician in her first year of practice who lacked confidence in herself and doubted her clinical skills. I saw a caring and compassionate doctor who was stuck in patterns of thought and behavior that were actually creating the very job and life she didn't want. And so I began by reassuring her that I knew how to fix what was wrong in her life. And then we started with mindfulness.

Developing the skill of being mindful is the first step in feeling better and taking action to create a better career. Mindfulness is a way of noticing what is happening right now.

Again, my favorite definition comes from Jon Kabat-Zinn in his book *Full Catastrophe Living*. He writes that mindfulness is "the awareness that arises by paying attention on purpose, in the present moment, and nonjudgmentally." (4)

Physicians have very busy minds. And our minds like to focus on the negative: what is wrong, what can go wrong, what has gone wrong. We're trained to do this, right? We are trained to look for problems even where none exist. This has helped us as a species survive until now and helps us be good doctors, but this is not contributing to our happiness or fulfillment. These negative thought loops often run in the background, and until we become aware of them, they create a low level of anxiety, worry, and uncertainty that we might even assume is normal.

Often, we are so busy thinking that we miss out on what is actually happening right now. You might notice you are so caught up in thinking about your workday that you don't even remember taking a shower or making coffee. You were essentially on autopilot: your body went through your morning routine while your mind was already at work. Such mind wandering seems normal, and it is – the human mind does wander, a lot. Why is this a problem? One reason is that when you aren't paying attention to the present moment, you miss out on the good moments in your life as well as the bad. Have you ever come back from vacation and felt like you were so distracted thinking about work you sort of missed out on your leisure time? Or finished eating and realized that you didn't even taste the food? A recent study published in *Science* found that a wandering mind is an unhappy mind. Matthew A. Killingsworth and Daniel T. Gilbert found that people were less happy when their minds were wandering than when they were not, and this was true during all activities, even during the least enjoyable ones. (5) This suggests that bringing awareness and attention to every part of your day will directly contribute to your happiness.

The first mindfulness tool I teach my clients is how to use awareness to create a brief time-out for themselves. This is especially useful if they are feeling overwhelmed by their feelings or a situation at work or home. It is also a great way to strengthen the muscle of self-awareness. The tool is STOP. It is easy to remember the steps:

S = Stop
T = Take a breath
O = Observe
P = Proceed

Simple, right? I like to break it down a little more, especially if you are unfamiliar with mindfulness techniques. Please try it now. It's fine to read about mindfulness, but it's not the same as actually doing it, just as describing what honey tastes like never compares to actually tasting honey.

So once again, STOP – this time try it yourself:

S = Stop what you are doing. By interrupting yourself, you can pause and gain more awareness of what's happening inside.

T = Take a breath (or two or three). Try to notice the physical sensation of breathing: from the movement of air coming in through your nose or mouth to the feeling of your chest or abdomen rising and then falling and finally the feeling of air leaving your body.

O = Observe what is happening. This may include observing what you are feeling and thinking as well as what you are sensing. Try to specifically notice what you are seeing, feeling, tasting, smelling, hearing. Can you?

P = Proceed with what you were doing before.

What was this like for you? It's normal to feel awkward or weird or to wonder whether you are doing it right. You are. There is no wrong way to observe yourself and what is happening around you and inside you. Although you might notice some self-critical or self-judgmental thoughts and feelings, this is normal, too. Later on we will work on changing that negative self-talk, but before you can change anything, you have to be aware of it.

The STOP tool is simple and easy, and yet it allows you to truly become aware moment to moment in your life and to develop the ability to experience any moment, no matter how intense or difficult, with more ease and equanimity. You may wish to incorporate this into your day. Maybe you can practice this in between seeing patients or surgical cases. Or use an app to prompt you to STOP a few times randomly during the day. Try it and see what happens.

Developing a mindfulness practice is really as simple as stepping into the role of observer over and over again. I call this being the Watcher. When I am the Watcher, I watch my thoughts and emotions. It is sort of like watching clouds float by in the sky or the ticker slide by at the New York Stock Exchange. You are just noticing them go by. You don't have to get involved in the thoughts or emotions. You don't need to evaluate them or judge them. You just observe them. And allow them to be there. And allow them to leave. You just watch them, almost as if they were someone else's thoughts and feelings.

You may notice you have a tendency to try not to think a certain thought or feel a certain emotion. This is common and normal. But it creates resistance. And resistance equals stress.

You can even practice being the observer by noticing your resistance and allowing your resistance to be there just as it is.

You may want to try this right now. Can you become the Watcher? What are you thinking and feeling right now? Pause here and spend a few minutes just noticing your thoughts and feelings.

What did you notice? Did you notice any resistance to what you observed yourself thinking and feeling? What did that resistance feel like in your body? Were you able to allow the resistance to be there?

Just keep practicing noticing and allowing. You may even want to say it out loud. It might sound like:

"I'm thinking that I hate my job."
"I'm thinking that this is stupid."
"I'm feeling irritated."
"I'm feeling impatient."
"I'm feeling hopeless."

Does it feel different to you to consciously notice these as thoughts and feelings rather than just thinking and feeling them? Stepping into the Watcher role often has the effect of creating a little space between you as the observer of your thoughts and feelings and those actual thoughts and feelings.

This is the beginning of defusing painful thoughts and feelings, or de-fusing from them.

Viktor Frankl is often cited as the source of this powerful observation: "Between stimulus and response there is a space. In that space is our power to choose our response. In our response lies our growth and our freedom." This is what we are cultivating here. It is the whole point of this practice of mindfulness and becoming the Watcher of ourselves. Again, before we can change anything, we need to become aware of it. Through awareness and the habit of allowing and accepting whatever we are currently experiencing, no matter how intense or painful, we create that space and give ourselves the power to respond more skillfully and in ways that will bring us the results we want in our careers and lives.

Happiness Hack 1: Meditate Your Way to a Happier You

Meditation may sound woo-woo or too touchy-feely or weird for you. But the science is in! Meditation increases gray matter in your brain, improves mood and makes you feel better, decreases stress-related cortisol, strengthens the immune system, and helps with a variety of medical conditions. (2, 6) If I could encourage you to start doing one thing right now that will benefit you so much in the long run, it is to start meditating. I grew up with meditating parents but "rebelled" against it myself for many years. However, a few years ago I rediscovered meditation for myself and now also teach it in the form of mindfulness-based stress reduction (MBSR). I cannot tell you how valuable my meditation practice is to my health, happiness, and ongoing well-being, and I have seen it help my clients as well.

A powerful tool for increasing your happiness level is engaging in a few minutes of meditation each day. Studies suggest that just two minutes a day is enough to see (and feel) measurable benefits.

Happiness Hack: Set a timer for two minutes. Sit in a comfortable and yet alert, upright position. Sit, and know you are sitting. Gently close your eyes and take a deep breath in and release it. Let yourself set aside any worries or concerns for the next two minutes. Turn your attention to your breath, breathing normally and naturally. There is no need to control your breath; just let it be what it is. Turn your awareness to the sensation of breathing. Maybe you notice the sensation of air passing in and out of your nose. Maybe you notice the rise of your chest or abdomen with each inhalation, and then the gentle falling with each exhalation. Try to stay with each breath from beginning to end. If (and when) you discover that your mind has wandered, that is fine. Notice what your attention has wandered to, and then let it go. No need to beat yourself up. This is what the mind does. It wanders. Just return to your breath. Bring your awareness back to the sensation of each breath. Allowing each moment to be as it is. Feeling your breath come and go, like the rising and falling of the ocean. When the timer signals the two-minute mark, gently take one final breath. And thank yourself for taking this time to contribute to your own health, happiness, and well-being. Gently open your eyes and resume your day.

Well-done! How was it? Now you can say you have meditated. I encourage you to set aside a couple minutes a day and keep practicing. Try it for a few weeks and see what you think, and, more importantly, see how you feel.

CHAPTER 5

You Have to Believe it to See it

"A man is but a product of his thoughts.
What he thinks he becomes."

– GANDHI

Step 2: Identify Your Thoughts

In the last chapter you practiced becoming aware of your thoughts and feelings, of moving into the observer mode. In the second step of the MINDFUL process, you get more practice identifying your thoughts and beliefs and understanding how powerful they really are. As Shakespeare famously wrote in Hamlet: "There is nothing either good or bad, but thinking makes it so." Do you believe this? I hope that by the end of this chapter you see that it is true.

Let me demonstrate the power of our thoughts and mind. Imagine you are holding half of a juicy lemon. Really picture it. Feel the weight of the lemon in your hand. Notice the texture of the rind. Imagine the smell of lemon rising up in the air. And now I want you to imagine biting into that lemon. Taste that sour lemon juice on your tongue.

What happened? Did you notice how you started to salivate? Did you feel your tongue and mouth pucker at the taste of the imaginary lemon? That is how powerful our thoughts are. That is how the mind can create such a vivid "fake" narrative. And we respond to it as if it is real. That is the power of a thought.

The field of positive psychology is fascinating, and much of the recent research supports this idea that how we feel, specifically how happy we are, has very little to do with the circumstances of our lives and much more to do with our internal narrative and view of our past, present, and future. In fact, one researcher, Sonja Lyubomirsky, has conducted research that suggests only 10 percent of variance in happiness is from the circumstances in our lives. (7) Think about other physicians you know. Some are happy and some, in almost identical jobs, are unhappy. Why? Really take a moment and think about it. How is this possible? This is so important. We think that to be happier, we first need to change something in the outside world (job, career, partner, etc.). But we don't. This doesn't mean that we don't change the outside world but that we do it knowing that it is not going to make us happier per se.

I want to introduce you to a coaching tool that changed my life. It is a way of understanding and solving any problem you might have. A spiritual teacher of mine, Byron Katie, is the author of the book *Loving What Is*, and it was she who first explained that the way to understand my life and everything in it is by understanding the way life works. And the way to understand anything in life is to understand the cycle of Think; Feel; Act; Have.

So, you think something and that causes you to feel something, and then you take action (or fail to act), and those actions give you the results that you see in your life.

Then I met the brilliant life coach and owner of The Life Coach School, Brooke Castillo, who is another very important teacher and mentor of mine. She had created a similar tool, called the Model, based on her study of many teachers, including Byron Katie. The Model is an elegant way to solve any problem. I use it every day for me and my clients. It lets you very clearly understand why you feel the way you do and why you have, or don't have, the career, life, or results that you want to have in your life.

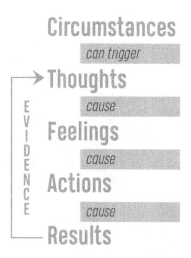

The way I like to explain this is by looking at a negative or unwanted result a client has in life. Perhaps a job they don't like or the burnout they are experiencing or not having any free time for themselves. Rather than just encouraging this client to take new action to change the results they currently have, we start by examining what they are thinking that is causing them to take the action (or inaction) that is creating the result they currently have and don't want. This is critical. You first need to understand why you have a certain result in your life, and only then will you be able to take effective action to change it permanently.

A good example of using the Model is Dr. M. She says she is unhappy in her job in large part because she is on call seven days a week for her surgical patients. I could have coached her to take action to change this right away, but without understanding the thoughts behind that result, any change is typically temporary and relies on willpower. After all, she is smart. She probably knows some ways to change this. And yet the situation is not changing. I have clients all the time say they want to work less, and yet they just keep overworking. Nothing changes. I asked Dr. M. why she was on call all the time and her answers (thoughts) included:

"I have to because it's in my contract."
"No one else can do it."
"I'm a surgeon and that's always part of the job."
"Everyone else takes call for their own patients."
"I don't want to seem lazy or entitled."
"It's unrealistic to expect to not have to take call."
"They might fire me if I try to change it."

These are all thoughts she is having that cause her to say yes to call rather than to honor her true desire, which is to take less or no call. These thoughts, once identified, can be questioned and disbelieved. Better thoughts might be:

"I can change my contract."

"There are other surgeons who might be able to take call."

"I don't have to do what everyone else does. I can choose what works for me."

"Not taking call is not lazy or entitled."

"There are doctors, including surgeons, who don't take call."

Then I helped her find evidence to support these new beliefs and to start practicing them. Once she started believing these new thoughts, it was easier and natural to take aligned action to create the new result she wanted, which was less call.

But even before doing that, we worked on getting her to feel better about her call schedule *before* changing it. This is so important. This is how you start to really understand that how you feel is based not on the facts of your life but on how you think about the facts of your life. Pause here. I am going to repeat this because it is so critical: *how you feel is not based on the facts of your life but is based on how you think about the facts of your life.*

To see this and practice this, I had Dr. M. do what I call a thought download on all of her thoughts about being on call seven days a week. A thought download is when you write down every thought in your head for five minutes. Don't edit. Don't judge. Just write. Then I had her do the following two exercises to see how her thinking about being on call was the actual cause of her negative emotions and of the results she was getting in her life.

The fact is that she is currently on call (home call) for her patients seven days a week. Her thoughts about that include the following:

"It's not fair."
"I never get a break."
"It's too much."
"I hate it."
"I can't take it."
"I never want to be on call again."

These thoughts make her feel terrible. When we went through the exercises, she discovered that these thoughts made her feel angry, sad, resentful, bitter, unhappy, and powerless. And none of these feelings were helping her to take more effective action to change her call schedule, which is what she really wanted. Then we looked at other thoughts she could have about being on call. I have a friend, a plastic surgeon, who is on call all the time and doesn't mind it a bit. I borrowed some of his thoughts for her to "try on." These thoughts included

"Being on call is no big deal."

"Taking call is just part of my job."

"I get paid for taking call."

"Sometimes I don't get called at all."

These thoughts, if she believed them, would cause her to feel much more positive emotions: calm, contented, happy, not bothered. See how that works? The key is finding thoughts that feel better to you *and* that you can believe. Dr. M. worked on thinking, "I get paid for taking call" and "I can negotiate to stop taking call." With the first new thought she felt a bit better while on call, and the second new thought helped her feel empowered to take action to change her call schedule permanently.

Going back to the Model, circumstances are facts. Facts are neutral. Facts are provable. They include what people do and say, what happens in the world, anything that could be proven in a court of law.

Thoughts are essentially sentences in our head. They are what we think about the circumstances (facts) in our lives. Thoughts are optional. And beliefs are simply thoughts we think a lot. Many of my clients spend time trying to figure out why they believe something. I don't think this is useful. We all have thoughts and beliefs we got from our families of origin, from our culture, from our peers, and from our past experiences.

What is more helpful is to notice whether our current thoughts are useful or not. Are our thoughts creating what we want or creating more of what we don't want?

Many of my clients tell me so-called facts that are actually just thoughts. They think they are simply telling me how it is. It might sound like this:

"My boss is unsupportive."

"My patients are demanding and unappreciative."

"Patients should respect my time and not be late."

"I don't have time to take a vacation."

"It's impossible to finish my charts at work."

"I hate my job."

"I feel miserable all the time."

These seem true. These beliefs feel true to my clients. And that is because they believe them. But are they really facts or are they thoughts? And what are the results of thinking these kinds of thoughts over and over?

What are some thoughts you are very used to thinking? Think about your job or career for a moment. How would you describe it? Notice whether you are simply describing the facts of your job or if you are including a lot of opinions and thoughts that might seem like facts to you. Are your feelings about your job caused by the facts of your job or your thoughts about it? It's tricky, isn't it? And it's very worthwhile to spend time on this to see your patterns of thoughts and beliefs in action.

How Thoughts Become Habits

> *"Thoughts believed create your world. When you question your thoughts, you change your world."*
>
> – BYRON KATIE

One reason it is so important to become aware of our thinking is that our thoughts create our feelings, and then our feelings drive all our actions. It is estimated that we have about sixty thousand thoughts a day. We have too many thoughts to regulate all of them, but we can bring awareness to these thoughts as much as possible, especially the ones that are causing a lot of our suffering. An unsupervised mind is like a toddler with a knife. We need to pay attention to what we are thinking and believing if we want to feel better and create the career of our dreams. Our mind is an amazing tool, but often we let it run the show. One of my favorite sayings is "The mind is a wonderful servant but a terrible master." This is so true. How often do you feel like your mind (and thoughts) are in charge of you, not you of them? As you recognize thoughts for what they are – just sentences in your mind – you take back all your power. Just because you think something doesn't make it either true or useful. You, the observer of your mind and thoughts, are the one in control. You get to use your mind; don't let it use you!

Common thoughts that seem true and useful but that are not either typically include "have to" or "should" or "must." These thoughts are never true. They seem true, and we act as if they are true. But really, pick one thing you believe you "have to" do. A common one I hear from my clients is they "have to go to work." When you believe that, how do you feel? Maybe powerless, angry, or unhappy? But ask yourself, is it really true that you have to go to work? Is someone forcing you to do it? Isn't it more accurate to say that you are choosing to go to work? Ask yourself why you might be choosing to go to work. Maybe your reasons include you want to have money, you want to support yourself or your family, you have patients who need you. Identifying the consequences of not going to work might help you see why you are currently choosing to go to work. How does it feel to recognize that you are choosing to go to work rather than having to go? Usually, it feels much better. And it is only by taking 100 percent responsibility for your choices that you can then decide to make a different choice that is more in line with what you truly want in your career and life.

The Inner Critic and Negative Self-Talk

As you continue to practice noticing your thoughts, especially in challenging or upsetting situations at work, you will likely notice a lot of self-critical and downright mean thoughts about yourself. If you are anything like me, this inner mean voice might sound like:

"You should be able to handle this better."

"You are so selfish."

"You should feel grateful for even having a job."

"How can you be unhappy? You are a dermatologist, for goodness sake."

"You got yourself into this mess. You are the only one to blame."

"You don't know what you're doing."

Whatever the self-critical thoughts are, you will notice them because they sting – a lot. They are typically thoughts you would never say to another person, or at least not to someone you like at all. The answer is not to beat yourself up more for having these thoughts and for being unkind to yourself. They don't mean you have low self-esteem. This is normal. These are just thoughts. They don't mean anything. We all have this inner critic. That voice is actually trying to help. Our brain is always looking for danger, looking for mistakes, trying to protect us, and trying to avoid pain. Our doctor conditioning likely exacerbates this tendency.

There are several ways to effectively manage saying mean things to yourself about yourself. I find the best response is simply to say, "Thank you for sharing," or "Your opinion is noted," and move on. It doesn't have to be a big deal. Another technique I like is to imagine that critical inner voice as a radio station or TV channel and imagine turning the volume down. You don't have to turn it off (and you can't), but it doesn't have to be so loud. The third option is to simply decide that you will have a zero-tolerance policy for being mean to yourself. Just like we don't tolerate bullying in our schools, you can set this policy for yourself. It takes practice, but gradually a lot of this habitual negativity simply extinguishes itself.

Here are some questions you can ask to get a better sense of your inner critic and change the negative inner dialogue:

What are some common thoughts you tell yourself that are mean or that you would never say to someone else?

Why are you being mean to yourself? How do you think this inner dialogue is helping or hurting you?

Can you make a commitment to try the techniques for abolishing negative self-talk and see which work best?

Practice this daily. You will slip up – and that's okay. It is a practice. It takes time to establish new habits of talking to yourself in a positive tone.

Another powerful and surprisingly difficult tool is to list twenty things you like about yourself. Bonus points if you can list fifty or a hundred. These can be small or big, but just turning your attention to what you like about yourself can cause powerful ripple effects. Can you mentally list some things you like about yourself right now? Or grab a piece of paper and a pen and write them down. That is even more powerful. Many of my clients can find only a few things they like about themselves. Or they feel uncomfortable and boastful when they list them. What is the experience like for you? Is it hard or easy?

The "Victim" Story

One of the biggest problems I see physicians have in general, especially my unhappy doctor clients, is playing the victim. Most doctors don't even realize they are doing this. I certainly didn't realize this about myself for many years. And I was in complete victim mode for much of my adult life. You will know you are in a victim mind-set whenever you find yourself complaining, justifying, or blaming. These complaining, justifying, and blaming thoughts are poison – poison to you and to your ability to take effective action to start creating a career and life you love.

The victim mind-set is defined as blaming your challenges or life circumstances on others. Basically, it is not taking 100 percent responsibility for your life. Yes, a lot that happens in life is beyond our control. How we respond to the events of our lives, however, is under our control. Accepting responsibility for that is empowering. And it can be frightening. Complaining can feel good. But complaining will keep you stuck. Use that energy to take action rather than disperse it with "venting." Don't vent. Do take action to change what you don't like, or if you can't, to change how you think and feel about it.

However, do pay attention to what you want to complain about. This shows you what you care about and what you want to change (and feel as if you can't). Complaining is good information on where you might begin the process of redesigning your career and life. Notice who you blame and for what. How can you start taking full responsibility for this instead? What are you really wanting in your life? And how can you make it happen?

This will change everything for you. Really. But don't take my word for it. Try it out for yourself and see.

Happiness Hack 2: Cultivate an Attitude of Gratitude

Numerous studies show the positive benefits of consciously cultivating an attitude of gratitude. What we focus on grows. What we pay attention to – the thoughts we think – determine how we feel. Practicing gratitude is a shortcut to feeling better every day. By consciously looking for the positive, we counteract the tendency of our brain to focus on the negative.

Happiness Hack: Every morning when you wake up, think of three things for which you are grateful. Pick new things every day. They can be as simple as "running water" or "a hot cup of coffee." Bonus points for writing them down. Maybe get yourself a special gratitude journal and keep a list. Spend two minutes really thinking about these three things. Notice how it feels in your body to feel grateful.

Optional: if you prefer, you could do this on your drive home or at lunch or before you go to bed or any other time. Pick a time that acts as a trigger reminding you to cultivate gratitude every day or program a reminder into your phone or calendar.

CHAPTER 6

Feelings are for Feeling, Not for Fleeing

"Feelings are just visitors, let them come and go."

– Mooji

Step 3: Navigate Your Feelings

This chapter is quite possibly the most important chapter in this book. And it is about something almost all of my physician clients don't want to talk about – feelings. I get it. As doctors, we have been taught to hide our feelings, ignore our feelings, and suppress our feelings. Or at least this is what I was taught. If not out loud, it was certainly modeled for me in medical school and residency.

But this doesn't work forever – feelings have a way of not being ignored. I know this from personal experience. I tried to ignore my feelings my whole life. It doesn't work. In fact, getting in touch with your feelings and learning to process them are the keys to getting what you truly want in life.

What Are Feelings?

As with anything, it is important to understand what something is and what it is not. Feelings (or emotions) are information. (I use the terms *feelings* and *emotions* interchangeably. Some researchers differentiate among the terms *emotions*, *feelings*, *moods*, and *instincts*. However, for our purposes, that level of detail and differentiation is not necessary.) As physicians, we know that, at the most fundamental level, feelings are the result of biochemical reactions in the brain and body. However, I find it useful in working with feelings to think of them as vibrations in your body. Feelings are always felt in the body. A feeling can be described in one word, such as glad, mad, sad, or afraid. Feelings start in your mind and travel to your body. They differ from physical sensations like hot, cold, hunger, and pain in that sensations come from the body and travel to the mind, whereas feelings start in the mind and travel to the body.

It is common to struggle with identifying your feelings. This is especially true for physicians, many of whom have spent years, if not decades, suppressing their feelings. If you have a hard time identifying what you are feeling, try asking yourself if you are feeling sad, mad, glad, or afraid, or something else. You don't have to make it complicated; one word is perfect. The following is the first tool I use with clients to help them identify their feelings. You can do it right now while you read this book.

What are you feeling now? (Describe it in one word, such as sad, mad, glad, afraid.)

Where is this feeling in your body? (Common locations include your chest, throat, and abdomen.)

What does it actually feel like in your body? (Describe it like you would to an alien who has never felt an emotion.)

What color is this feeling?

Is this feeling hard or soft?

Is this feeling fast or slow?

What does this feeling make you want to do?

Why do you think you are you feeling this?

Did you notice anything about the intensity of your emotion as you went through the exercise? As we turn toward our feelings and identify and describe them, we step into the observer mode. We become the Watcher again. Just like when we observe our thoughts, this creates a little space between us, the observer of the feeling, and the feeling itself, which allows us to defuse the intensity of the feeling. This is one reason it is so beneficial to pay attention to how we feel, specifically in a curious and nonjudgmental way.

Why Are Feelings Important?

Understanding and identifying your feelings are important because feelings are the reason you do everything (or nothing) in life. Everything we do is because of how we think it will make us feel (happy, excited, safe, content). Everything we don't do is because of how we think it will make us feel to do it (ashamed, guilty, embarrassed, afraid). Think about it. You studied hard in school because you wanted to feel accomplished or successful or to make your parents proud. You became a doctor to feel successful, kind, compassionate, and caring. You are reading this book because you feel miserable or confused or stuck. And you are hoping to find answers that will allow you to feel happy and confident and sure of yourself and your future.

So, understanding what feelings are is very important. But it is also important to understand what feelings are not. Feelings are not facts. Feelings are not dangerous. Feelings can't harm us. Feelings can't kill us. Feelings are not who we are but just something we experience. Feelings are not forever; they come and go and change over time. In fact, the natural time course for an emotion or feeling state in our body is approximately ninety seconds. Feelings last longer only when driven by repetitive thoughts. Knowing this can give us a sense of control over our emotions and take away some of the fear of strong feelings overwhelming us.

Take a moment and ask yourself which are the top three negative emotions you avoid or resist feeling daily. What do you think might happen if you let yourself feel them? What is the worst thing that might happen if you allow yourself to feel one of these feelings? When you think about this feeling and everything you've done to avoid feeling it, can you explain why you've tried to avoid it so much? A simple vibration is harmless in our body, so why do we do so many things that might be harmful to ourselves to avoid it? If you were willing to feel this emotion without fear, how might you act differently in your life? What might you do differently and why?

What Causes Our Feelings?

It seems like our feelings are caused by outside events, people, and the circumstances of our lives. For example, my clients often complain that they feel irritated because their patients are rude. Or they feel overwhelmed because they have too much to do. Or they feel frustrated because patients don't follow their instructions and are wasting their time.

This is what we are taught growing up. We were all told not to say unkind things to others so as not to hurt their feelings. Or a well-meaning parent or teacher asked us if someone hurt our feelings and made us feel sad. But, actually, our feelings are internally caused. Always. Our feelings don't come from the outside world. Our feelings are caused by what we *think* about the outside world. This may seem like a small point, but it is huge. Understanding this can change everything for you. It did for me.

Let me illustrate this with an example. A client was upset and frustrated after clinic. (See how a feeling can be described by one or two words?) I asked her why, and she said it was because her patient didn't use the medicine she had prescribed and was wasting her time and didn't value her expertise. My client thought she was upset by the patient not taking the medication. But what I pointed out was that she was upset because she was making that mean the patient was wasting her time and didn't value her expertise. If she had thought something else, such as "Sometimes patients don't do what is best for themselves" or "He must not understand how important it is to take this medicine as prescribed" or "Maybe the medicine was too expensive," my client would likely have felt a different emotion, such as curiosity or concern. What do you think feels better? Frustration and upset or curiosity and concern?

The reason this is so important is that if our feelings are caused by our thoughts, it means we are 100 percent responsible for how we feel. *This is such good news!* This means that other people do not have the power to make us feel a certain way. This means that although we cannot control what happens in the world, including other people's behavior, we can control what we make it mean and, therefore, how we feel. Don't just take my word on this – test it out.

Understanding that the feelings you feel come not from outside circumstances or events but rather from your thoughts and beliefs about those events gives you authority over how you feel on a daily basis. Notice your feelings, and they will lead you directly to the thoughts you are thinking. This is critical because it allows you to take 100 percent responsibility for how you feel. You don't have to leave your career, or even change your career, to start feeling better. You can start feeling better right now. Once you really understand this, it will change everything. And this doesn't mean you won't still want to change your job. Feeling better first actually makes it easier to change whatever you want to change about your job or career. This is because your actions will be motivated by positive feelings (like excitement or enthusiasm) rather than negative emotions (like fear or despair). Which feelings do you think would help you find the job of your dreams? Feeling excited and enthusiastic or afraid and despairing?

How to Feel a Feeling

It seems sort of silly, but so many of us don't know how to feel a feeling. Learning to allow your emotions and to process them is a skill most of us physicians need some help with. And learning how to allow your feelings also gives you much more authority over them. When you aren't afraid of them, negative emotions lose a lot of their power. Feeling your feelings does not mean having to act on them or express them. It is an internal process that you can do at any time, in any situation. It's like doing a Kegel exercise. No one has to know.

We can deal with or respond to feelings in four ways: resist, react, avoid, and allow. The first three of these responses are not useful or helpful, but they tend to be the most common responses I see in my clients.

The first way many of us respond to negative feelings is to resist them. Resisting an emotion is like trying to hold a beach ball under the surface of the water. It takes a lot of energy and, in the end, the beach ball pops up to the surface anyway. Resistance looks like feeling angry while telling yourself you shouldn't feel angry and pretending you don't. It may look like feeling impatient and yet trying to act as if you have all the patience in the world. It actually makes the emotion feel bigger. We often resist an emotion because we worry it will overwhelm us if we allow it, and yet the opposite is true. By resisting it, we give it much more energy and perpetuate it. Rather than lasting ninety seconds and then fading away, when we resist a negative emotion, it usually persists much, much longer.

The second common way we respond to our unwanted emotions is to react to them. Reacting to emotions may include acting on them or expressing them. This is typically not useful or helpful. Yelling or screaming is not the same thing as feeling our feelings. It may seem that we are "releasing" something or processing our emotions, but really we are simply acting them out. We may find ourselves identifying even more with them and making our feelings into a really big deal. Processing or feeling an emotion doesn't look like acting them out or expressing them. Rather, it is something that happens internally when you are experiencing the physical sensations or vibrations of that particular emotional state.

The third way many of us deal with negative emotion is simply to try to avoid it. Common ways we avoid emotions are by overeating, overdrinking, and overworking. Other avoidance techniques can look like anything done to excess or to "distract ourselves," especially those that trigger a dopamine rush in our pleasure and reward centers in the brain. These might include shopping, excessive social media use, binge-watching TV or movies, pornography, and simply being "too busy" all the time.

What I recommend learning to do is to *allow* any emotion you might be feeling. This is the fourth way to respond to emotions. Allowing emotion is how we feel our feelings and process them in a healthy and empowering way. What does allowing look like? It is simple, but not always easy. Let me walk you through one way of allowing or processing an emotion without resisting it, reacting to it, or avoiding it.

Right now, ask yourself these questions:

What am I feeling?

Where is it in my body?

How do I know I am feeling this feeling versus a different feeling?

What is specific about this one?

Can I allow it more room?

Can I relax into it? Breathe into it?

Is it changing? Does it feel different?

Try this a few times. Don't rush through it. This is something you can, and should, practice. Again, you may notice that as you move into being the Watcher, you no longer *are* your emotion but rather are the one experiencing it. Even telling yourself, "I am not angry. I am the one experiencing the anger," may help you create a little space between you and the feeling you are experiencing.

It is like allowing anger or fear or whatever emotion you are feeling to have a room in your house. You can open the door and go in and experience the feeling while knowing you can leave at any time. This skill means that you can handle any emotion you might experience. And knowing this gives you confidence to allow yourself to grow and go after your dreams. Right? If you know how to allow yourself to feel fear, shame, embarrassment, or whatever feeling you most avoid, what could stop you from going after any goal, no matter how big? Once you realize that a feeling isn't going to kill you, and you know how to feel it and what is really causing it, you have so much more power.

How to Practice Creating Feelings

Once I discovered that my feelings were caused by my thoughts, I was naturally in a hurry to start changing my thoughts so I could feel better. That makes sense, right? My clients do this, too. It's normal. And I think it can be a useful skill to have. Once we get the hang of allowing our feelings, it is not such a big deal to experience negative emotions. And it's normal to feel some negative emotion. There are times we might want to feel sad or angry. And yet, sometimes it is nice to know how to interrupt the pattern and feel better at any time.

One-Minute Emotional Makeover

This is one of my favorite tools to use and to teach my clients to use. Again, practicing this is important. See if you can try it now, or the next time you are feeling upset or angry or sad, come back to this section.

1. Describe what you are feeling in your body (describe the physical sensations in detail, as if you were explaining them to an alien who has never felt any emotion).
2. Name the feeling (for example, "I am feeling sad" or "mad" or "glad" or "afraid").
3. Identify the thought/sentence in your head that is causing this feeling.
4. Change the thought to one that creates a better feeling.

One of my clients completed this exercise as follows:

Describe what you are feeling in your body.
My chest feels sort of tight and hollow. My throat is dry. I feel a little queasy and my stomach feels like butterflies or like it's really unsettled.

Name the feeling.

I feel anxious.

Identify the thought/sentence in your head that is causing this feeling.

I don't know what my long-term career plans are.

Change the thought to one that creates a better feeling.

I am figuring out my career plans, and I have plenty of time to do so. (This made her feel more in control and relaxed.)

As with any new skill, practicing the technique will make you better at it. It might feel awkward at first or seem too easy, but try it and see how it works. Test it at work and at home, and let your results encourage you to keep experimenting with creating the feelings you want to feel more often.

Feeling Mastery

Congratulations! You now know more than the vast majority of people about feelings and how to feel them, what they are and what they are not, and how to change them. You definitely know way more than most other physicians. Knowledge is power. Use this knowledge to help yourself understand how you feel at any given moment, why you are feeling that way, and how to change your feelings so you can get the results you want. This is so important because it allows you to feel better right now. And once you feel better, even in your current job, you will realize that you have many more options than you currently see. What is the main reason you haven't made any changes yet? Probably because of a feeling like fear or uncertainty or confusion. But now you know what is really causing those emotions (a thought), why those feelings aren't a big deal, and how to change them (change your thinking and only then take action).

Happiness Hack 3: Let the Good Inside

This is a simple two-minute exercise that has been shown to increase our happiness quotient quickly. It works by counteracting our negativity bias. Focusing on and really dwelling on a positive experience minimizes the natural tendency of our brain to be "Velcro for negative experiences and Teflon for positive ones."(2)

Happiness Hack: On your drive home from work, think about a meaningful and positive experience or interaction you had today. This could be a return patient who came in much improved and said thank you. Or a word of praise from your boss. Or even a pleasant walk you took outside at lunchtime. Really focus on the details of the experience. Focus on the feeling of it. How do you feel in your body when you reflect on this experience or interaction? For two minutes dwell on the feelings and sensations this memory evokes. Bonus points for sharing this out loud with a loved one or friend. The more you focus on positive and meaningful events in your life, especially reliving the emotions and sensations that accompanied the event, the more they become a permanent part of you.

CHAPTER 7

Live Your Life,
Not Someone Else's

"Your time is limited, so don't waste it living someone else's life. Don't be trapped by dogma – which is living with the results of other people's thinking. Don't let the noise of other's opinions drown out your own inner voice. And most important, have the courage to follow your heart and intuition. They somehow already know what you truly want to become. Everything else is secondary."

– Steve Jobs

Step 4: Determine Your Values and Priorities –
Live Your Life, Not Someone Else's

I remember the day I realized that although my life was great on paper, it didn't feel great. And it didn't feel great because it wasn't the life I really wanted to be living. It was the life I *thought* I should be living. It felt like I was trapped in someone else's life. And I didn't want to be there anymore. Have you had this experience, too?

Looking back, it made sense. I was so used to following the path that was laid out in front of me by other people. In college, I picked a major and fulfilled the graduation requirements without questioning them. In medical school, it was very clear what I needed to do to graduate and become a doctor. So I did it, and when the going got tough, I just worked harder. In residency, it was the same thing. I did what was expected of me and more. I followed the rules and made it through. Then, I actually did consider what I wanted from my first job. I chose to work four days a week rather than five. But I didn't really question much else. And many of my clients don't either. They just accept what they are offered without checking to make sure it is what they truly want.

We often don't realize that, once we are out of training, our career path and our lives and our daily schedules are really up to us. We get to choose. And if we don't choose, someone else will choose for us. And this is really the benefit of getting to the low point where you are now. Physician burnout and deep unhappiness with your career do help us in the end, as long as we navigate them well and with enough support. Often, we need to hit bottom (or near bottom) to see that we must make some changes. Most physicians have a very high tolerance for pain, and this is why I see so many doctors reach out only when they are in so much pain and so desperate to feel better that they seriously consider leaving medicine. That is often the only option they see. It's my job to help them see all the other options they have too, all the many paths they can take, in medicine and in life. There is no one-size-fits-all medical career.

The first step to getting on your path is to identify what your values and priorities are. When I ask my clients to describe their values, they are usually stumped. This is not something we reflect on regularly. But knowing your values, and living a value-guided life, is how you create a life of joy and fulfillment.

Your values are what you judge to be important in life – in your life. Values are how we navigate our lives and the choices we make, even when we are faced with setbacks and tough situations. Values are different from goals in that goals are very specific and can be accomplished or achieved. Values are something we can always live by, regardless of the circumstances. Making $1 million a year is a goal. It can be achieved. It is very concrete. Financial values, on the other hand, are being self-sufficient, providing financially for loved ones, and being of service. They are not something you ever finish. You want to set goals that are in alignment with your values (we will get to that in a later chapter), but first you need to identify what your values are.

Identifying Your Values

You can identify your values by asking yourself these questions and taking the time to answer them:

"Deep down, what is really important to me?"
"What sort of person do I want to be?"
"What do I want my life to be about?"
"What kind of relationships do I want to have?"
"What do I think the purpose of my life is?"
"What makes my life worth living?"

A lot of my clients struggle to answer these. If you are struggling as well, think about people you admire. What are the characteristics you admire in them? These are likely your values. Who are the people you don't admire? What are their values? Yours are probably the opposite of theirs.

The next step is to see where you are living in line with your values and where you are not. I want you to think about your last few days. What did you spend your time on yesterday? And the day before? What proportion of your time and energy went toward people, work, and things that you really value? How much does your day-to-day routine reflect your true values and priorities?

This can be a real shock to my clients. Many of them are living way out of alignment with their stated values. But the good news is, once you see this, you can't unsee it. And you can start living more in alignment with your values right away. That's because values are applicable to any situation.

My client Dr. G. had a value of being physically healthy and active. In reviewing her day-to-day life, however, she realized she was eating poorly, not sleeping enough, and not getting regular exercise. She was able to live more in alignment with her value of health and wellness by going to bed earlier, making better food choices, and walking around the hospital in between clinics to get exercise in her daily routine.

Another client, Dr. M., realized one of her values was being a caring and compassionate person. She realized that her behavior at work with patients and staff was neither caring nor compassionate of late. She was in fact taking out a lot of her frustration and burnout on those around her. I reassured her that this was actually a symptom of burnout and a sign of hitting bottom as an unhappy physician, and it didn't mean that she was a bad person or doctor. As she began to see that she was in charge of her life and focused on what was working in her job, she also began to take time for herself and her own well-being. Then she naturally began showing up as more of the caring and compassionate person she wanted to be and truly was at heart.

What are some changes you can make to live more in alignment with the values you listed above? Can you commit to implementing just one small change this week?

Chapter 8

Self-Care Isn't Selfish

"Self-care is never a selfish act – it is simply good stewardship of the only gift I have, the gift I was put on earth to offer to others."

– Parker Palmer

Step 5: Fuel Yourself First – Self-Care Isn't Selfish

How many physicians do you know who are good at prioritizing their own well-being? They don't work too much and they get enough sleep and make time for exercise and downtime and they have a healthy lifestyle. Not many, right? There is something about the very idea of prioritizing yourself that seems to fly in the face of being a "good" doctor. And this is why burnout and exhaustion and overwork are such problems in today's medical world. And why so many physicians are considering leaving their medical practice or retiring early. That is exactly why self-care is not selfish.

Taking care of you *is* taking care of your patients. Any conflict you perceive here is a misperception. The mantra I learned in my medical training, however, and the one I even taught to my residents, was "the patient always comes first." Somehow, this also seemed to mean that my own needs and well-being came last. This is such a problem that the new Hippocratic Oath (or "Declaration of Geneva") now includes this clause:

"I will attend to my own health, well-being, and abilities in order to provide care of the highest standard."

Are you attending to your own health and well-being?

What Self-Care Really Is

> *"You can't pour from an empty cup.*
> *Take care of yourself first."*
>
> – UNKNOWN

What is self-care anyway? On social media it appears mostly as getting massages, or pedicures, maybe a nice meal, a girls' night out, or just a very large glass of wine after a hard day. Yes, these can be self-care activities, but more superficial ones, in my opinion. True self-care is often really challenging. It may be saying no to seeing a late patient, it may be not baking cookies for your child's school fund-raiser, it may be cutting back your work hours or going to bed on time rather than zoning out with Netflix. Self-care is really about prioritizing your well-being so that you can then be of service to the world in whatever ways you wish to be. Self-care is not easy. If it were, you would already be doing it. Right?

You must become your top priority. You are your number one. I coach my clients all the time on why they must not sacrifice their own physical, mental, and emotional health for the sake of anyone else's... ever. If someone really needs you, they need you to be healthy and available. Once you start taking care of yourself, you will discover you have so much more to give to others. It really is a win-win situation. Again, taking care of you *is* taking care of your patients, family, and loved ones. Not taking care of yourself is depriving the world of what you are here to accomplish. It is procrastination in doing your work in the world.

Typically, my clients discover the reason they are not taking care of themselves is because they are putting others ahead of themselves. Remember the instructions on the airplane: put on your oxygen mask first before helping others with theirs. This includes your children, your family, and your patients.

It can help to understand why you are putting other people's well-being or happiness ahead of your own. Can you remember a recent situation when you put another person ahead of yourself? What are some of the reasons you did this? Can you see how, right now, you are more willing to disappoint yourself than others? Are you willing to disappoint others in order to not disappoint yourself? Why or why not?

Until you are willing to disappoint other people rather than yourself, you will continue to be depleted and likely feel resentful. Resentment and irritation are signs of poor or nonexistent boundaries. Setting healthy boundaries can prevent a lot of unnecessary friction. A boundary is *not* a way to control other people. A boundary is a way of protecting yourself. It may seem like boundaries separate us from others, but they really do quite the opposite. A boundary includes a request you make of someone to change a certain behavior, and a consequence of what *you* will do to protect yourself if they violate the boundary again. The boundary includes what you will do, not what *they* have to do. There are two steps to set an effective boundary:

1. The request: Ask someone to stop doing something that infringes on you or your property.

2. The consequence: Tell the person what you will do if he or she does not comply.

An example is a patient who yells at your staff. You ask this person to stop yelling, and then you tell him that if he doesn't, you will discharge him from your practice. Or you tell a chronically late patient that if she cannot show up on time, you will ask to have her rescheduled and she will not be seen that day.

People Pleasing Won't Make Your Dreams Come True

"A dishonest yes is a no to yourself."
– Byron Katie

So many of us physicians are chronic people-pleasers. Again, this is normal. But it is not contributing to our happiness or to creating a life that is our own. We are social creatures, and the threat of not being liked is a very primitive fear. It probably goes back to the fact that centuries ago, being exiled or isolated from others usually meant death. I believe we still have this instinct to get along, be part of the group, make sure other people are happy, and make sure people like us. There is nothing wrong with wanting these things. The problem is when we say yes to others at our own expense. When we do this, we are lying. We are providing bad information. We are setting ourselves up for martyrdom and resentment.

Ask yourself honestly if you tend to be a people-pleaser. Do you say yes to things you don't want to do to make (or keep) others happy? Are you worried people won't like you if you were to speak and behave more honestly with them? Do you feel like you need outside validation and the approval of others to feel good about yourself? How much do you worry about people seeing you as lazy, uncaring, selfish, or totally egocentric if you were to do what you actually wanted to do? Most physicians answer yes to all of these. I used to as well. I still struggle with letting people think whatever they want about me. (Hint: they will anyway.) For so many years I deferred my dreams because I was so worried about making other people happy.

There is nothing wrong with wanting other people to be happy. If doing things for someone in your life brings you happiness and doesn't come at your own expense, go for it! Just make sure that you are not placing someone else's happiness and well-being above your own. You are not responsible for making anyone else happy. And, in the end, you can't make other people happy. Have you ever done something you didn't want to do to please someone and then gotten angry when they weren't happy with it? So frustrating, right? Typically, we just want other people to be happy so we can be happy. And because we can't control how other people feel – because how they feel is caused by their thoughts – I recommend cutting out the middleman and making yourself happy. Typically, when you are happier, those around you are happier, too. Your being happy sets other people free to be happy. Being a happier physician leads to a better working environment and probably to happier, and healthier, patients. Being a happier spouse or a happier parent likely makes every aspect of your life and your loved ones' lives better!

One of the most powerful, and difficult, exercises I have for my clients is practicing giving an honest yes or no. Identify one recent situation when you said yes in spite of wanting to say no.

What were your reasons for saying yes? (Go back and notice what you were thinking just before you said yes.)

What are the reasons you wanted to say no?

Which reasons do you like better? Which reasons feel more like love?

Can you practice not saying yes when you want to say no?

Don't Let Busy Steal Your Life

So many of my clients and, let's face it, pretty much everyone else, are always saying they are busy. "Too busy." But busy is a choice. Busy is often an excuse. We all have the same amount of time. Are you spending it in the way you wish to? Why or why not? This ties in to the values you identified in the last chapter.

What is busy to you? What does busy look like for you? Can you make a mental list of what typically keeps you busy? What is really important on that list? Is there something else you actually want to be doing with your time? I challenge you to practice saying no to those things that you don't want to do and that are not really important. See if you can delegate some of those tasks or outsource them or maybe just delete them altogether. Start small, but definitely start.

Next time you find yourself saying you are too busy to do something, I want you to rephrase your answer more honestly. If you find yourself saying you are too busy taking care of your kids to work out, I want you to say, "I am choosing to make my kids' needs more of a priority than my own." Or "I am choosing to watch movies and lie on the couch rather than go to bed on time." Of course I want you to have plenty of time to spend with your kids and time to watch Netflix. I just want that time not to come at the expense of your well-being. How can you do both? Usually the answer is to say no to things you truly don't want to do and don't value.

Learning to say no is a skill. As Oprah says, "No is a complete sentence." Typically, we say no and then give a bunch of excuses. Or we say yes and then feel resentful that the person even asked. Any time you think someone shouldn't expect you to do *x*, *y*, or *z*, I want you to flip it around. Isn't it truer to think that *you* shouldn't expect yourself to do *x*, *y*, or *z*? Why are you expecting that? Other people are allowed to ask. We are allowed to say yes or no. Really.

Practice saying no. Practice with your spouse or partner. Practice in the mirror. Practice in less-risky situations like at the grocery store or coffee shop. As you complete the next exercise, you will have lots of opportunities to say no.

Schedule Your Life on Your Calendar First

If you do only one exercise in this book, do this one. And do it every week. This is the most important thing you can do to prevent burnout and ensure that you feel happier and more fulfilled and enjoy your life more. Doing this recharges you so that you have more energy and enthusiasm for your work and for the rest of your life.

What I want you to do is schedule your nonwork priorities. Put anything you want to do on your calendar. Preferably do this with the people you live with: spouse or partner, kids. This way, everyone can be involved and you can create a family calendar as well as a personal calendar. You can do this either in a calendar app or on a paper calendar that you then take a photo of with your phone. It must be on your phone! If you can't refer to it and keep track of what you have planned, those activities likely will not happen. Having your calendar on your phone also allows you to check it when someone at works asks you to switch call or work late or attend a meeting. You can't wing it. If you aren't already keeping a calendar like this, this is why you currently don't have enough free time set aside for you.

Start blocking out time for you and your family and other loved ones. Do this every week or every month. Events you must include on this calendar are the following:

- Fun activities that help you relax or recharge, such as gym time, yoga, running, dance classes, hiking, swimming, massage, pedicure
- Movie time or TV time
- Free time (maybe block off an afternoon or a whole day to devote to anything or nothing)
- Time with friends and family
- A weekly or biweekly date night
- Time to schedule the next week or month on the calendar

One of the secrets to having more free time is to block it off on your calendar in advance. Whenever possible, block off your free time and fun time before you schedule your work activities. And then you can do whatever you want to do in that saved time. This can include spending time with your family or enjoying solo time. Scheduling time off in advance actually allows you to be much more spontaneous in the moment. Try it and see.

This calendar needs to be on your phone so that when someone asks you to do something, you can pause and say, "Let me check my calendar." And then you check your calendar. If you have something scheduled on your personal or family calendar, you tell them no. You can say no in many ways:

"I have a prior commitment."
"I'm not available."
"I'm not free then."

You don't have to give details, but it is also fine to simply tell the truth: No, that is my time with my kids or my date night or my workout class. It's up to you. This will probably be really hard. And it is also so valuable to strengthen your self-care muscle and get comfortable saying no. Practice this! Role-play with your kids or partner. Make practicing saying no fun and natural. And then honor your calendar.

Ask Better Questions to Get a Better Life

Asking better questions has been a game-changer for me and my clients. Asking a better question of yourself can make all the difference between staying stuck and moving forward. We ask ourselves questions every day. Our brain not only is a thought generator but also excellent at finding the answers to the questions we ask ourselves. Our brain can find evidence for anything. It is like a well-trained lawyer – it can argue for the prosecution or the defense. What I want you to do is notice what kinds of questions you are asking yourself and whether they are useful. Use your brain to find creative and new solutions for the problems you face in your life.

Unhelpful questions are those that keep you in a negative thought and feeling loop. We might not even realize it, but most of us have done this before. The kinds of questions that have no upside to asking include these:

"Why is my life so hard?"

"Why am I so unlucky?"

"Why doesn't anything ever go right for me?"

"Why can't I find a job I like?"

"What's wrong with me?"

"Why did I make the mistake of becoming a doctor?"

"Why do I have to work so hard?"

"Why can't something be easy for a change?"

See how these presuppose a negative outcome? And so your brain is just going to go find evidence for why this is true. And we always see what we are looking for. If you look for what is wrong in your life, and why it can't get better, you will most definitely find it.

Good questions are ones that help you feel better and take positive action to go after what you want. Good questions if you are an unhappy doctor with a job you don't like might include these:

"How can I have a good day today?"

"How can I make sure I get home on time today?"

"What is great about my life today?"

"What is good about this job right now?"

"Why am I choosing to go to work today?"

"How can I make today better than yesterday?"

"How can I make more money today?"

"How can I best be of service today?"

"How can I enjoy this job more?"

"What can I do to make this job a better fit for me while I figure out my long-term plans?"

You get the idea. Notice how the answers to these questions are going to lead to more positive feelings and to taking action to create more of what you want.

What questions do you ask yourself every day? Can you start asking a better question? If you don't allow your brain to come back with "I don't know," you will find a source of wisdom within you that you might not have realized existed. The higher quality the question is, the higher quality the answer will be.

This is a trial-and-error process. See what works. See what doesn't. Self-care seems so simple. But if it were, we all would have lives with much better work-life balance and integration. The fact that so few physicians make time for their own wellness and happiness speaks to how challenging this is for us. And also how important it is to change what is not working in your life now. If you do what you've always done, you'll just keep getting what you've always gotten. Or as it's said: "Insanity is doing the same thing over and over and expecting different results."

Please do these exercises. Especially the calendar one. If you want to change the results you are getting in your life – and I think you do – you must take action. It will feel uncomfortable. But everything you want in your life is waiting for you outside your comfort zone.

CHAPTER 9

Dream, Baby, Dream

*"The great secret of getting what you want from life is to
know what you want and believe you can have it."*

– NORMAN VINCENT PEALE

Step 6: Uniquely Yours – Identify
Your Dream Career

Are you focused on your past or your future? Most of us are past-focused. We think about the choices we made, we might regret things we did or did not do, and we wonder about other potential paths we didn't take. Being past-focused, however, keeps us stuck in the past and likely repeating it. This chapter is about turning your attention to your future and creating a future that is so much better than your past.

The degree to which you don't know what you truly want is the degree to which you won't ever get it. Many times we are so busy simply surviving our busy lives as physicians that we don't ever stop to consider our dreams. We believe we will never be able to get what we want, so we consider thinking about our dreams as frivolous and unrealistic. You have kids and a mortgage after all, right? But I assure you, it is not frivolous or unrealistic – it is, in fact, required. Within you is your very own map to your destiny, and it is written in your wants and your desires. Pay attention to what you want and to what you truly desire, and you will start living the life you are meant to be living. As the poet Rumi said, "What you seek is seeking you."

This is when it gets fun! This is when you give yourself permission to want what you want. To dream big. And then to dream even bigger! To be totally unrealistic. To not censor yourself. To not worry (yet) about *the how* but to start by focusing on *the what*. It is also very common and normal to feel a little scared or vulnerable when you write down your dreams and what you want. For so many years you have been telling yourself you can't have what you really want or that you need to be "realistic" and "make the best of it." So, plan on it feeling uncomfortable when you crack open that long-sealed door to the basement room where you exiled your dreams.

I have my clients start by identifying their top five (or ten) life goals. What are five things that you feel like you must accomplish or experience in your life before you die? What would you, on your deathbed, deeply regret not having experienced? These might change in time or after you have achieved some of them. It is good to revisit this exercise at least yearly. Examples from my clients are as follows:

To have a life partner and an amazing loving and passionate relationship.

To become a parent.

To be an amazing mom to my children.

To have a job that I love going to every day.

To have a deep connection with God.

To have a job in which I earn enough to start a foundation for my charitable causes.

To travel to every continent on the planet.

This is an exercise that I encourage you to do on paper. It is helpful to write it out and revisit it. Post your answers where you can see them regularly.

List your top five (or ten) outcomes for your life.

Think about how you spent the last few days. How much of your time was used to help make your top priorities become a reality? (Please don't use this information to beat yourself up. This is just about getting clear on why your life is not fulfilling.)

List some things you can do that might contribute to making these top outcomes a reality.

Put this list somewhere you can see it every day.

Knowing What You Want

The biggest mistake I see unhappy physicians make, and that I made myself (and that cost me a lot of money), is to leave their current job before they know what they want. I hear this all the time. My clients tell me, "I don't know what I want, but I do know I don't want the job I have now." And that is fine – knowing what you don't want is often the first step to change. But it is much easier, and much more efficient, to identify what you want rather than to keep focusing on what you don't want. In fact, focusing on what you don't want is a problem because it not only keeps you feeling terrible but also prevents you from taking effective action to find the job you want and the life of your dreams. But you can use knowing what you don't want to help you determine what you truly do want.

Let's start by having you identify what you don't want. Can you make a mental list of everything you don't like about your job? Feel free to think about current and past jobs. Then think about everything you don't like about your current career and being a doctor in general. Last, think about everything you don't like about your life in general. This is sort of a bummer to do, isn't it?

It is also rather easy. But it is crucial not to get stuck here. As I mentioned before, the more we focus on what we don't want (and currently have), the more negative we feel about our lives and the less likely we are to take action. It is counterintuitive, but test it yourself. When you think about everything you don't like about your job and career and life, how do you feel? Maybe depressed or angry or hopeless? When you feel that way, what do you do? Typically, when we focus on what we don't like about our lives, we either don't do anything or we do something to distract ourselves and make us feel (temporarily) better. This might be having a glass of wine, eating a cupcake, watching TV, going shopping, or complaining. None of these lead to change.

So now think about what you *do* want. This is incredibly important. Again, knowing what you want is the road map to where you want to be headed. You need to know where you want to go before you start. Think about it like taking a road trip. You are in Chicago. Do you want to go to New York City or San Francisco? There are many routes to either place, but you need to know your destination first. Then you can start to figure out how to get there.

One thing I notice is that many of my clients use gratitude to keep themselves stuck. Feeling grateful is a wonderful emotion that we can cultivate by expressing appreciation for what we have. Positive psychology studies have recently shown gratitude increases our well-being and happiness and is associated with increased energy, optimism, and empathy. That's why I included cultivating gratitude as a Happiness Hack. However, many physicians tell me they aren't happy, but they don't feel like they are allowed to be unhappy because they already have so much: a loving partner, kids, a good job, and so forth. This is what I call the gratitude trap. Yes, I want you to absolutely appreciate what you have. But don't let having a "good" life stop you from going after more. Wanting more doesn't make you selfish. Wanting more is part of the human experience. Wanting more is how we evolve to the next level.

This exercise of listing what you want will be very powerful and important for you if you tend to use gratitude as a way of staying stuck and feeling sort of "blah" in your life. You might be one of those physicians who isn't super unhappy, but you aren't really happy and definitely are not excited about your future. Be grateful and let yourself dream: what else might you want to achieve or go after or experience in your life?

Grab a piece of paper and a pen and write down fifty things you want. You can include things you want that you already have (like a spouse or children or a house). Include big and little wants, maybe vacations, experiences, dreams. If you can't write it all down now, just go ahead and do it in your mind.

Was it hard to come up with fifty things you wanted? Was it easy? How do you feel now? Some of my clients feel energized. Many clients, however, feel either depressed or sort of selfish and greedy after completing this exercise. This is good information. Because we know that our thoughts create our feelings, go inside your head and figure out what you are thinking about this list you just made. Maybe you think it's too much? Or that you shouldn't want so much? Or that you should be more grateful for what you do have? Or maybe you think that this list is just pointing out everything you don't have and that you will probably never be able to fulfill these wants. It is really important to identify your beliefs about your future and what is possible for you.

What do you believe about your future? Many of my clients are so deep in survival mode that they haven't asked themselves what they really want because it seems so futile and painful. Shifting your beliefs about what is possible for you and your future is essential to creating the future you want, even if you currently think it might be too good to be true.

Take a moment and simply reflect on the following questions:

What do you think your future will look like?
How do you feel when you think about your future?
How do you want to feel about your future?
What would you have to believe to feel that way?
Can you believe that now?

A lot of my clients think they are simply telling me the truth about their future. They don't realize that they are actually telling me their thoughts about their future. And that those thoughts might not be useful or true. And that those thoughts are all optional. Let me share with you some of my thoughts about my future. And feel free to borrow them:

"I have plenty of time to do what is truly important to me."

"My life is always getting better and better."

"I will always keep learning and growing into the next version of me."

"I can create whatever I want in the future."

"I want to help make the world a better place now and for the future."

Ideal Job Description

Now that you have gotten in touch with some of your life goals and made a list of your wants for your life in general, let's work on creating a specific vision of your ideal job. The hardest part of this is not to get stuck in the "yeah buts." The "yeah buts" are those negative comments your brain so helpfully (not really) provides whenever you start to dream or think about making changes in any part of your life. The bigger and more important the dream, the more your brain panics and tries to warn you that it's impossible and that you should just give up now. This is normal. This is your brain, your primitive brain, trying to keep you safe.

Our brain evolved to keep us safe. It wants us to avoid pain and seek pleasure. It wants us to stay in the cave (safety) and not venture outside (danger). And until the pain of your current job or life situation gets too intense to bear, your fear of change is often successful in keeping you "safe" and stuck right where you are. That is why so many doctors accept their current job "as is" and try to "make the best of it" rather than change it to better suit them or find a new job altogether. The fact that you are reading this book tells me that your pain is finally enough to urge you to overcome the fear of making changes. So, congratulations on having the courage to come this far. It will only get better from here, I promise!

On a nice piece of paper with a favorite pen, start writing down a description of your ideal job. Or do it on your computer. I just want you to do it. I often have my clients label this their "too-good-to-be-true" job description. Sometimes just acknowledging that this is an "ideal" or "too-good-to-be-true" job helps quiet that voice of the inner critic and the "realistic" part of your brain.

Now ask yourself whether you still enjoy clinical practice. Do you still enjoy seeing patients or operating or medicine in general? Most of the physicians I work with discover that they genuinely do enjoy parts of their medical practice but that the parts they don't like are draining all the joy out of being a doctor. If this is you, do the exercise in terms of describing your "too-good-to-be-true" clinical practice. If you truly don't want to stay in clinical medicine at all or see patients, this is when you write down your ideal job description outside of medicine.

I want you to be as specific as humanly possible. If your brain keeps telling you that something is "unrealistic" or "silly" or "impossible," just say, "Thanks for sharing," and keep going. This is why I call it your "too-good-to-be-true" job description. This exercise usually takes days or weeks to do and is a work in progress. It is not something you do once. As the circumstances in your life change (marriage, baby, illness, new interests, etc.), your ideal job description will change. What is it now?

Start by remembering why you went into medicine in the first place. How did you picture your life as a doctor? When you were deciding which residency to pursue, what patients did you imagine yourself taking care of? What was your vision for your practice and your career? If you could have it all your way, what would your ideal medical practice look like? Here are some prompts to answer along the way:

- Patients: Do you want to see patients and, if so, what kinds of patients with what kinds of diagnoses? Do you want to do procedures and, if so, which ones? If you don't want to see patients, which work activities do you enjoy?
- Additional jobs and/or income sources: Any interest in leadership roles, research, consulting for pharmaceutical companies, clinical trials, selling products in offices, cosmetic practice, teaching, administrative roles in hospital or group practice? Do you want a side gig?
- Setting: Office, OR, hospital; one site or several? Do you want to work from home or to travel? Work environment?
- Type of practice: Academic, private, combination, solo or group, small group, large group, employee or self-employed, teaching, volunteer or paid, telemedicine/virtual or in person?
- Colleagues: Do you want to be alone in the office or practice or have other colleagues, MDs, or midlevels such as PAs and NPs? Do you want to have medical

students or residents rotating with you? Communication style with colleagues and boss?

- Income: How much do you want to make? How much do you need to make at minimum to support yourself (and any family or dependents currently)?
- Practice financial structure: Cash pay, insurance paid, or both; on salary or on production or percentage, or both?
- Location: Urban or rural? What state or geographic area or international? What recreational activities are important to have nearby? Do you want to be close to family or not?
- Schedule: How many days and hours per week? Will it include nights or weekends? Will you take call and, if so, how often? How flexible in terms of sick days or family emergencies? How family-friendly and flexible do you need your schedule to be?

Again, if you genuinely have no desire to see patients, please do this exercise but answer it in terms of your ideal nonclinical job description. The same questions apply: day-to-day activities, location, work environment, work in an office or from home, hours and days and salary, travel, and so forth? Details are important.

This exercise is crucial and typically takes days or weeks to complete. Don't be in a rush here. You may want to put it aside and come back to it tomorrow to take another pass. There is no wrong way to do this. The only mistake is not doing it. You don't have to know how to make it happen; right now you just want to focus on getting clear about what your ideal job looks like. Your power to create this dream future increases dramatically with the clarity of your view.

Chapter 10

Lights, Camera, Action!

"Be careful what you water your dreams with. Water them with worry and fear and you will produce weeds that choke the life from your dream. Water them with optimism and solutions and you will cultivate success. Always be on the lookout for ways to nurture your dream."

– Lao Tzu

Step 7: Look Out for Obstacles and Problem Solve in Advance

This is the make-it-or-break-it chapter. And that is because until you start taking action, nothing changes. You will know when you have made a decision to change your life because you will start taking action. Until then, you haven't really decided.

The key to sustained change is small and steady actions taken over time. One mistake I see many of my clients make is trying to change too many things at once. And then they feel overwhelmed and quit. My first coach and teacher, Martha Beck, taught me the principle of "turtle steps." This is the idea of creating lasting change by taking the smallest step possible. You make the first step so easy that you can't possibly *not* do it. For example, say you want to start getting up earlier. If you "turtle step" it, maybe you start by getting up one or two minutes earlier every day. In a month, you are getting up thirty to sixty minutes earlier. One way you will know you haven't made the first step small enough is if you aren't doing it. Our doctor training tells us that big changes are better. But small changes add up to big changes in time, and we are much more likely to follow through with change if we make it as easy as possible. When in doubt, ask yourself how you can make it easier. This also goes against our medical doctor programming. And that is okay. Easy is often better than hard. Yes, you can do hard things. And you will. But don't do hard things just because they are hard. If you can do it in an easier way, do it.

In the last chapter you described your ideal job. Now I want you to compare your ideal job to your current job. How do they compare? What percentage of your ideal job's characteristics are present in your current job? Are they at 30 percent? Or 50 percent? Or 70 percent? Most of my clients come to me in the under 50 percent category, but sometimes a client is pretty satisfied with her clinical practice and just needs help in a couple of key areas. The goal is to get your current job to overlap as much as possible with your ideal job. I would aim for at least a 70 percent or 80 percent overlap. The good news is that you are probably not that far off your path. Just like sailing a boat, small changes can quickly take you in a very different direction.

Right now I am pretty sure you are saying that there is no way your current job can ever get to an 80 percent overlap with your ideal job. And I hear you. That's what you believe and that is why your current job is not better. That's why the next steps (and working with someone who can help you believe that change is possible) will be critical for you.

The next thing you must do takes some time, but it makes your success in creating change in your job much more likely. The goal is to make it impossible for you *not* to achieve the career changes you want. But when we are confronted with making changes or going after our dreams, especially if they feel big and important to us, our brain usually starts telling us unhelpful things, like this:

"I don't know where to start."

"This is too hard."

"This is never going to work."

"I should just quit now."

"This is a mistake."

"There is no way I can change my job."

"This is impossible."

You get the picture? This is what my brain tells me all the time. It is totally normal – and totally not helpful or true. That is why this exercise is so important. It allows us to use our big, beautiful, problem-solving brain to our advantage. You are a doctor. You solve problems for a living. You can absolutely do this! This is where your meticulous, look-for-problems medical training pays off in advance.

Mapping Out Change and Overcoming Obstacles

> *"If you want something you have never had, you must be willing to do something you have never done."*
>
> – THOMAS JEFFERSON

Start by looking at your ideal job description. Then make a separate list of everything that you must change about your current job to make it more like your ideal job. What would need to change? Again, be specific. Write every single thing down. Don't censor yourself.

For each change, describe why you want to achieve it. (For example, "I want to work three days a week to have more time with my young children.") Next, for each change, list all the potential obstacles to creating that change. This is when you get to use that "yeah but" brain of yours. (For example, if your goal is to get home by six every evening, what currently prevents you from doing that? Charting, call-backs, inbox, EMR, scheduling your last patient too late, last-minute add-ons, and so forth. Each one is a separate obstacle to your goal of getting home by six p.m.) And, finally, for each obstacle, brainstorm solutions in advance. Come up with as many potential solutions as possible. List each action step you would have to take. (For example, schedule your last patient at four p.m., not four-thirty. Actions include talking to your boss about changing the schedule, talking to office staff about the new schedule, and so forth.)

This is your personal map to a happier and more balanced practice and life. Now you have a list of specific changes that will make your current practice more like your ideal practice (your *what*). You have a clear list of why you want these changes (your *why*). And you have a clear list of all the obstacles to achieving these goals or practice changes and potential solutions (your *how*). Congratulations! You've done the hardest part.

Finally, I want you to pick one item on your list of changes to make to your current job. I would pick the easiest item. However, some of my clients prefer to focus on the one that would make the most impact in their life. It is up to you. I recommend picking the easiest change so that you can change it and move on, gain momentum and confidence in the process, and make it as painless as possible. Now put the steps you have outlined (the obstacles and their solutions) on your calendar. What is the first step? When are you going to do it? Put it on your calendar. And repeat for the next step and so on. Just focus on one change at a time. Do not move on to another change until you have been successful with the previous one. If you discover an obstacle you didn't foresee, that is fine. Just take a deep breath, and brainstorm solutions for it. Remember the principle of "turtle steps." Just keep going. The way to climb even the biggest mountain is simply one step at a time.

It can be so helpful to have support with this. This is challenging stuff. Make sure you have someone to check in with, strategize with, and get support from, such as a colleague, a coach, or a friend. How can you best set yourself up for success? How can you make your success inevitable?

A Word on Failure

> *"I have not failed. I've just found 10,000 ways
> that won't work."*
>
> – Thomas Edison

Failure. What does this word mean to you? How do you feel when you think of failure? I used to be so afraid of failure. I thought failure was bad. I made it mean so much about me. It was not until I read Carol Dweck's book *Mindset* that I realized I was looking at failure all wrong. If you have a fear of failure, or if you take failure to mean something negative about you, I highly recommend reading her book. Adopting a growth mind-set means learning to see failure as feedback. What would you be willing to do or try if you genuinely saw failure as an opportunity for growth and for learning something, not as something bad? You can change the way you see failure. The most successful people in the world fail their way to success. You can too. It's as simple as changing your mind.

CHAPTER 11

What If Becoming a Doctor Was a Mistake?

How to Know When to Quit

"Live life as if everything is rigged in your favor."

− RUMI

You might be like me and wonder secretly sometimes if going to medical school was a big mistake. This was a very painful question I asked myself over and over. And for many years, I thought it was a question that actually had an objective, factual answer. It doesn't.

What happens when we think that going to medical school was a bad idea or a big mistake? Our brain focuses on this and finds lots of evidence for why it *was* a mistake. And then how do you feel? I felt terrible. I felt angry with myself, regretful, trapped, and disappointed. And when I felt this way, I wasn't showing up as the best doctor I could be. I would be at work but wish I was elsewhere. Or I would spend a lot of time thinking about all the careers I "could have" pursued and fantasizing about them. But there were also a lot of times when I remembered all the things I liked about medical school and how much I enjoyed being a doctor. And then I would feel so much better: happier, enthusiastic, and interested in my patients and my practice. At times like these, I was essentially finding evidence for why going to medical school was not a mistake. But I felt really torn at times – I didn't know which thought was true.

Do you realize that "it was a mistake to go to medical school" is just a thought, and not a fact? That it can never be a fact? That it is always just going to be an opinion? And opinions (or thoughts) are optional? The only fact or truth here is that I *did* go to medical school. Just like you did. You also decided to go to medical school for a variety of reasons, as did I. And it probably took some hard work on your part to graduate. It's not just something that "happens." Once I understood that "it was a mistake to go to medical school" was just a thought I had about the fact that I attended medical school, I realized I could set myself free from this once and for all. I decided to try on the thought that going to medical school may not have been a mistake. And I asked my brain to start finding evidence for this belief. I found *a lot* of evidence. And then I tried on the thought "I made the right choice in going to medical school." I started finding reasons that might be true. That felt so much better. Believing this thought doesn't mean you don't eventually leave your medical practice or the field of medicine altogether. You can always do that if you truly want to. It just means you get to feel better right now about your decision to become a doctor. Try it for yourself and see. I want you to finish this book and know that you never have to believe that going to medical school was a mistake, unless you want to.

Thoughts about Your Past

Ask yourself again why you chose to become a doctor and go to medical school. What do you think about your decision to become a doctor? How do those thoughts make you feel? How do you want to feel about your decision to become a doctor and attend medical school? What would you have to believe to feel that way? Can you believe that now?

How do you think about your past in general? And is it useful? Many of us have had a lot of difficult experiences in our lives. Our pasts might be painful for us to think about. Maybe we think we made a lot of mistakes or did a lot of things wrong. Most of us wish our past could be different in some ways. But it doesn't have to be different for us to feel better about it. Right?

Because it is our thinking that creates our feelings. So, to feel better about our past, we just need to think better thoughts about it. It seems simplistic, but it works.

The past is over. It only exists as sentences in your head. Think about this for a minute. If you sustained a head trauma and had total and permanent amnesia, would your past still exist? Would it matter to you?

You get to decide how you think and feel about the past. I like to think that everything happened just as it should. I like to think that my past was perfect for me – that my past was just what I needed to become the person I am today. I like to think that my past made me strong. I like to think that my past can't hurt me.

What if you decided to believe that your past was perfect for you? That it happened exactly as it was supposed to and that there were no mistakes, just lessons and preparation? That it was always going to happen just as it did? It is such a waste of your emotional energy and life force to try to argue with your past. Can you stop fighting with your past and start focusing on creating a future that is so much better than your past?

How to Know Whether to Stay in Your Job or Leave and When to Decide

One thing unhappy physicians ask me all the time is, "Should I quit my job?" My answer is generally, "No," or "Not yet." When you are hating your job and doubting your whole career, quitting seems like the solution. And it may be the right decision for you in the end. But try to stay as long as you can. Let's get you feeling better first, let's make some changes to your current job and life that give you some relief right now, and then let's reassess. It's as if you came to the ED with a broken leg. Yes, we could amputate it immediately and that would solve the problem in one way. But there are other solutions that are less drastic and probably better in the end. I hope you can learn from my experience.

If they haven't decided to quit or actually quit already, over 80 percent of my clients end up staying in their current job or in another job in medicine. And they feel happy and fulfilled. They are no longer simply surviving, but thriving. We work a lot on identifying what they want to change about their job or career to have it better match their ideal job description, and then on creating those changes. I do also help some physicians find a new nonclinical position better suited to their ideal job description and long-term goals. In such cases, I still think improving the physician's current job while planning for the next is such an advantage.

You can use your current job as a springboard to your next job without having to be miserable in the meantime. Just knowing that leaving your job is always an option can bring you a lot of relief. You never have to stay in your job or even in your medical career. Change is always an option. I just recommend it as an option of last resort. Once you can get your current job to somewhere between 70 percent and 90 percent overlap with your ideal job, that is when you can consider whether you want or need to change jobs or even careers. This depends on what your ideal job description looks like and what your dreams for your future are like. In the end, it is completely up to you. The best reason to leave your job is simply because you want to – not to be happier or because you feel like you have to.

Seth Godin has a wonderful short book called *The Dip: A Little Book That Teaches You When to Quit (and When to Stick)*. In it, he talks about quitting and the opposite of quitting. The opposite of quitting, he says, is not "waiting around." The "opposite of quitting is *rededication*. The opposite of quitting is an invigorated new strategy designed to break the problem apart." (8) I agree. I call this going all-in or all-out. Being halfway in and halfway out is a terrible position in which to be. It takes immense amounts of energy and you waste it spinning in circles. You should either accept your current job (and work on changing it) or reject it (and find a better one), but don't just continue to tolerate it. Tolerating = stress. Stress = elevated cortisol. Elevated cortisol = nothing good. As a physician, you know this.

First, let me reassure you that there are no mistakes and that whatever decision you make, regardless of what it is, is the right one. Many times we look for answers outside of us, as if the "right" decision is written down somewhere, if only we could find it. Being willing to take action and move forward, however you move, is the essential choice. The only mistake is remaining stuck in one place. As my father the sailor would say, you can't steer a boat unless it is moving.

And Then This Happened...

Life is about change and movement and growth. There is always going to be "something" that comes up. Expecting that one day all will be smooth sailing for the rest of your life is probably not realistic. And would you really want your life to be that way? Think about your favorite movies or books. They are engaging and entertaining *because* of the ups and downs. Would you go see a movie in which everyone was happy and life was perfect all of the time? No. Neither would I.

In my life, when an unexpected challenge or situation arises, I like to remind myself that this is the nature of life and that something has not gone terribly wrong. I do this by repeating "and then this happened." It reminds me that this is not the end of the story but the middle. And that just as I have made it through other challenging situations, I can and will make it through this one.

Your Future Self

The following questions are designed to help you think about your future and what kind of legacy you want to create. Fast-forward twenty years and assume the perspective of your future self, who is right where you want to be. Have the future you give you advice for your life right now. What would your future self tell you to stop doing? What would you tell you to start doing? What guidance can your future self give you? What decision could you make today about your job and your career that you would least likely regret? This might sound sort of woo-woo or silly, but it is a very powerful exercise. It allows you to tap into your own inner knowing and deep wisdom, without triggering some of your current fears. I really hope you try it.

Conclusion

What you seek is seeking you.

– Rumi

What Is Next for You?

Again, let me say congratulations to you for having the courage to pick up this book and read it. I so hope that you have put some, if not all of it, into action. I know that even in your worst moments of misery or despair, there is a part of you, your wiser and best self, that keeps whispering to you that there was a better way. And that your life is meant for so much more than what you have been settling for until now. And I am so very much on your side. I want this for you, and for every other unhappy doctor out there as well.

Burnout or hitting rock bottom in your career is actually such a gift if you use it to your advantage. It is often the turning point where you finally get off the wrong path and onto your own right path. This is your time. You deserve it.

I have a dream of a world in which all doctors are happy and fulfilled and love their jobs and their lives. I want physician burnout to become uncommon rather than increasing in frequency every year, across every specialty. I want my fellow physicians to be examples for their patients and show them that it is possible to combine a successful and challenging medical career with a life of health, happiness, and wellness. This is my goal. This is my dream. And I am pursuing it one unhappy physician at a time.

It's hard for me to leave you here, on the cusp of this, the beginning of the rest of your life. It may seem odd to say, but I feel that in some way I know you already. And I so fiercely want you to succeed in turning your life and career around. I remember all of us in medical school on that first day. I remember looking around and feeling both nervous and proud to be among my fellow students. Becoming a doctor was such an arduous process, and yet it is one that I honestly don't regret. It has been such a worthwhile endeavor. And I want to tell you, to reassure you, that even if you never practice again, you will always be a doctor. For, you see, we bring everything with us. Nothing goes to waste. I know this for a fact. And I want you to know it too.

In this book, you have everything you need to succeed in creating the career of your dreams and the work-life balance you want. I hope you will use it. I know you can succeed. Just keep going.

Bonus:

Two-Minute
Happiness Hacks

These Happiness Hacks are included earlier in this book, but this cheat sheet groups them in one place for convenience. Feel free to put them into practice right now.

Each one of these Happiness Hacks is based on scientific studies.

Each one requires only two minutes a day.

I recommend you start with one and commit to it for the next thirty days.

Happiness Hack 1: Meditate Your Way to a Happier You

Set a timer for two minutes. Sit in a comfortable and yet alert, upright position. Sit, and know you are sitting. Gently close your eyes and take a deep breath in and release it. Let yourself set aside any worries or concerns for the next two minutes. Turn your attention to your breath, breathing normally and naturally. There is no need to control your breath; just let it be what it is. Turn your awareness to the sensation of breathing. Maybe you notice the sensation of air passing in and out of your nose. Maybe you notice the rise of your chest or abdomen with each inhalation, and then the gentle falling with each exhalation. Try to stay with each breath from beginning to end. If (and when) you discover that your mind has wandered, that is fine. Notice what your attention has wandered to, and then let it go. No need to beat yourself up. This is what the mind does. It wanders. Just return to your breath. Bring your awareness back to the sensation of each breath. Allowing each moment to be as it is. Feeling your breath come and go, like the rising and falling of the ocean. When the timer signals the two-minute mark, gently take one final breath. And thank yourself for taking this time to contribute to your own health, happiness, and well-being. Gently open your eyes and resume your day.

Happiness Hack 2: Cultivate an Attitude of Gratitude

Every morning when you wake up, think of three things for which you are grateful. Pick new things every day. They can be as simple as "running water" or "a hot cup of coffee." Bonus points for writing them down. Maybe get yourself a special gratitude journal and keep a list. Spend two minutes really thinking about these three things. Notice how it feels in your body to feel grateful.

Optional: if you prefer, you could do this on your drive home or at lunch or before you go to bed or any other time. Pick a time that acts as a trigger reminding you to cultivate gratitude every day or program a reminder into your phone or calendar.

Happiness Hack 3: Let the Good Inside

On your drive home from work, think about a meaningful and positive experience or interaction you had today. This could be a return patient who came in much improved and said thank you. Or a word of praise from your boss. Or even a pleasant walk you took outside at lunchtime. Really focus on the details of the experience. Focus on the feeling of it. How do you feel in your body when you reflect on this experience or interaction? Dwell on the feelings and sensations this memory evokes for two minutes. Bonus points for sharing this out loud with a loved one or friend. The more you focus on positive and meaningful events in your life, especially reliving the emotions and sensations that accompanied the event, the more they become a permanent part of you.

I have one additional bonus Happiness Hack. It does take longer than 2 minutes however, but studies also show how beneficial it is!

Happiness Hack 4: Exercise for Happiness

Make a commitment to engage in fifteen minutes of light cardio a day. This does not need to be intense cardio, but it should involve some movement. Do something you find fun or pleasant, like walking, hiking, running, cycling, swimming, or dance.

Acknowledgments

This book has been a long time in coming. It is the book I wish I had years ago when I was navigating the challenges of my own medical career dissatisfaction and unhappiness.

I have been fortunate to have so many wonderful teachers and coaches and mentors. Thank you for shining a light for me in my darkness.

Martha Beck and Brooke Castillo, thank you both so much for sharing your knowledge with me and turning me into a bona fide life coach! I owe you both so much and am so grateful for everything you have each taught me. Because of you, my life has never been the same.

Bev Barnes, thank you for finally getting me off the island and into my boat!

Thank you Meadow DeVor, for your coaching, mentoring, and especially your friendship. It is such a privilege to have you in my life.

Angela Lauria – thank you so much! I knew when I decided to work with you that you would not let me fail. Thank you for your belief in me and my message and for keeping me always writing in the right direction. This book would not have been possible without you.

Where would I be in life without my wonderful teacher, Byron Katie? Thank you for your message and work in this world. I cannot imagine living without "The Work" being alive in my life.

Before I had real-life teachers, I had my books. I grew up with books as some of my best friends. They still are. Whenever I am in doubt or need help, I turn to a book first for answers. Thank you to each and every author who has sat down and written a book that made a difference in my life or someone else's. I have too many favorites to name. Seriously. Come see my house!

I am lucky to have so many amazing friends! Thank you for all your support, especially as I have lost and then found myself again in these last few years. Bari Cunningham, Collin McShirley, Jennifer Gray, Anu Jayaraman, Diane Murphy, Lori Logan, Eric Parlette, Christine Worden, Jim Hickey, Brent Cavender, Greg Feldman, Fred Krawchuk – thank you for your friendship. It means the world to me. And to my coaching partner for the last five years, Jennifer Sherwood, thank you for all your coaching, support, and friendship!

To all my wonderful coaching clients: you are so amazing and it is such a privilege to work with you. Thank you for trusting me to help you find your own path and learn to trust your own inner guidance to find and live your best life.

To all my SMD sisters. You know who you are. Thanks for the inspiration and love.

To the Morgan James Publishing team: Special thanks to David Hancock, CEO & Founder for believing in me and my message. To my Author Relations Manager, Bonnie Rauch, thanks for making the process seamless and easy. Many more thanks to everyone else, but especially Jim Howard, Bethany Marshall, and Nickcole Watkins.

And last but not least, thank you again to my dear family. To my mom and dad (Sally and Evan), to my sister Anna, my Uncle Peter, Aunt Susan, and to all my cousins, thank you so much for your love and support. It has been more important than you can imagine.

And of course, thank you, Mr. Tucker. You have been my loyal companion for all these years. No one could have a better dog than you!

THANK YOU

Thank you dear doctor so much for reading this. The fact that you've gotten to this point in the book tells me something important about you: you're ready. You're ready to feel better, improve your current job, and create a step-by-step plan to create your dream career and life. I want to help in any way I can!

To support you in taking action to quit being miserable as a doctor and identify what is specifically holding you back from feeling better now and finding your ideal job, I have gathered together some resources for you.

The Doctor Dilemma Checklist

You can download the free Doctor Dilemma Checklist at my website, doctordilemma.com. The checklist will help you get a sense of how unhappy you are in your current job and why, what level of burnout you might be experiencing, and what steps in the MINDFUL process you need to focus on to start to feel better, fix your burnout, and find your ideal job or career.

Free Strategy Session

I am always available for a free 30-minute strategy session to help you identify where you are stuck and map out your next steps. You can go here https://www.saradill.com/scheduling/ to schedule or head on over to my website at <https://www.saradill.com>.

Contact me

If you have a question or a comment or just need a virtual hug, feel free to send me an email anytime at sara@saradill.com. You are why I do this. I am happy to help in any way I can.

ABOUT THE AUTHOR

Dr. Sara Dill is a physician, life coach, and consultant who specializes in working with unhappy physicians struggling with overwork, burnout, and career doubt and dissatisfaction. She has degrees from Harvard, the UC San Diego School of Medicine, and Brown Medical School. She practiced in a variety of clinical settings for eight years as a board-certified dermatologist and sub-specialty-trained and certified pediatric dermatologist. Her positions included practicing dermatology at Brigham and Women's Hospital, Boston Children's Hospital, Brown Medical School Department of Dermatology/University Dermatology, Rady Children's Hospital, Kaiser Permanente in northern California, and in private practice. Sara spent two years as residency program director for dermatology at Brown Medical School, and it was during this time that she realized how much she enjoyed helping physicians, including residents and medical students, navigate the challenges of being a doctor and making wise decisions about their future careers and future life satisfaction. Since leaving her medical practice in 2012, she has experimented with locum tenens (Hawaii), started a business in food and wine, and worked as a medical director in clinical development for Allergan Pharmaceuticals, both full-time and as an independent physician consultant. Sara has tried every kind of practice known to physicians. This personal experience is the key to her ability to truly understand the experience of working as a physician and what works and does not work for unhappy doctors. After realizing her true calling is helping other doctors who are struggling with the demands of being a physician and the question of whether to stay in medicine, she has trained with numerous coaches and mentors, including Martha Beck, Brooke Castillo and The Life Coach School, and Byron Katie, and has spent years studying the science of happiness, positive psychology, career transition, and the steps to creating a life that matters. She now lives happily in Santa Barbara, California, with the world's laziest dog. The two of them recently returned from one of many cross-country road trips to the East Coast to enjoy the seasons (and lobster rolls) of New England.

Website: www.saradill.com

Email: sara@saradill.com

Facebook: https://www.facebook.com/sara.dill.73

References

1. John M. Gottman, *Why Marriages Succeed or Fail: And How You Can Make Yours Last* (New York: Simon & Schuster, 1995).

2. Rick Hanson with Richard Mendius, *Buddha's Brain: The Practical Neuroscience of Happiness, Love, and Wisdom* (Oakland, CA: New Harbinger Publications, 2009).

3. L. N. Dyrbye, C. P. West, and D. Satele, S. Boone, L. Tan, J. Sloan, and T. D. Shanafelt, "Burnout among U.S. Medical Students, Residents, and Early Career Physicians Relative to the General U.S. Population," Academic Medicine 89 (2014): 443–451.

4. Jon Kabat-Zinn, *Full Catastrophe Living: Using the wisdom of your body and mind to face stress, pain, and illness* (New York: Bantam Books, 2013).

5. M. A. Killingsworth and D. T. Gilbert, "A Wandering Mind Is an Unhappy Mind," Science 330 (2010): 932–932.

6. Daniel Goleman and Richard J. Davidson, *Altered Traits: Science Reveals How Meditation Changes Your Mind, Brain, and Body* (New York: Penguin Random House, 2017).

7. Sonja Lyubomirsky, *The How of Happiness: A New Approach to Getting the Life You Want* (New York: Penguin Books, 2008).

8. Seth Godin, *The Dip: A Little Book That Teaches You When to Quit* (and When to Stick) (New York: Penguin Group, 2007).